POSTCARDS
FROM THE
COSMIC CLUB
OF Everlasting Souls

POSTCARDS FROM THE COSMIC CLUB OF Everlasting Souls

VISITING HOURS ON BOTH SIDES OF THE VEIL

A TRUE STORY

MICHAEL GERRISH

PERMANENT PRESS PUBLISHING

Permanent Press Publishing
P.O. Box 13
West Newbury, MA 01985

Printed in the United States of America

First Printing, 2020

Paperback ISBN: 978-1-7349299-0-4
Ebook ISBN: 978-1-7349299-1-1

Library of Congress Control Number: 2020911583

CREDITS
Photographs throughout the book come from the author's personal collection. All rights reserved.

Custom typography and frontispiece artwork by Risa Rodil, risarodil.com

Book design by K. M. Weber, ilibribookdesign.com

To my muse, Marina Day.
With love and gratitude.

Table of Contents

☆

☆

*This story happened largely in the way
that it's portrayed. For clarity, some parts
have been adapted or condensed, but all reflect
the essence of what actually occurred.*

Visiting Hours

1

In the Beginning

My phone was pulsing fiercely on the table near my bed. I yawned, and turned to pick it up. The call was from my dad.

"Rise and shine," he said.

"The son will rise at noon," I quipped.

"Did I just wake you up?"

"No, Dad. I'm talking in my sleep."

"I'm sorry, what?"

"I said to leave a message at the beep."

I snickered, but the joke fell flat. He didn't say a word. He didn't even try to feign a semblance of a laugh.

"What's that noise?" he grumbled.

"Oops," I said. "It's my alarm."

"I thought you planned to rise at noon?"

"Hold on a sec, okay?"

While blindly stabbing buttons on my phone to quell the noise, I trashed an app, roused Siri, and snapped photos of my feet.

"Hello?" he huffed.

"I'm here," I growled. "This thing won't . . . there. It's off."

"It's what? I still can't hear you well. Repeat what you just said."

"What you just said."

"Say that again?"

"With pleasure. That again?"

"Quit the jokes, okay?" he snapped. "There's something you should know. Marina isn't doing well. Her doctor is concerned. Something happened, I'm afraid. You need to call her mom."

"Another setback?" I replied.

"Call Sharon. She'll explain."

There was a long, uneasy pause.

"What happened?" I exclaimed.

"Call Sharon," he repeated.

"Not Marina?"

"No. Not yet."

There was another lengthy pause.

"You're scaring me," I said.

"I didn't mean to," he maintained.

"Tell me what happened then!"

Again, my dad went silent.

"Did you hear me?" I inquired.

"Marina's had enough," he sighed.

"Enough?"

"She's giving up."

My stomach dropped. I groaned and shook my head in disbelief. I was aghast. So rattled that I couldn't even speak.

"Are you still there?" my father asked.

"In body," I replied.

"Are you okay?"

"Define okay."

"Marina asked for you."

TWO YEARS AND five months prior, all was well. Or so it seemed.

Although it still was early in the fall of 2010, the lush New England landscape glowed with vivid autumn hues. But the auspicious spectacle belied what lay ahead. The picture was about to change abruptly for my niece.

Marina Day was two months short of turning twenty-two. Pursuing dual degrees in music and performance art, her talent, wit, and winsome smile were sure to take her far. Poised to take the world by storm, she hoped to change it too.

About to start her third year at Bard College in New York, Marina was reflective while preparing to return. She missed her bright, fun-loving friends while on her summer break, and hoped to reconnect with them the moment she arrived. She also missed the college grounds and its eclectic charm. With modern structures flanking Gothic buildings clad in stone, the architectural pastiche is boldly avant-garde. And yet, as bold as it appears, it's in a fitting vein. The tenor is in keeping with the school's progressive bent.

With Bard three hours from Boston, and four hours from where I live, I didn't see Marina much except for during her breaks. I did, however, text her anytime she came to mind, and on occasion, called to get caught up on all her news. One day, though, what made me call was something less routine. I had a vague, uneasy sense that something was amiss.

"How's it going, kid?" I asked.

"I'm great!" Marina chirped. "I just danced my patootie off. What did you do today?"

"I farted in an Apple store. It was embarrassing. I would've opened windows, but I couldn't. Figures, right?"

"You're Microsofter than a grape!" She laughed. "What else you got?"

"My wit is lost on you," I sighed. "I'll quit while I'm behind."

Our breezy banter only put me slightly more at ease. I couldn't shake the feeling that I had before our call. On the surface, her good cheer appeared to be sincere, but failed to ease the feeling that was fueling my unrest.

An excerpt from Marina's blog explains what happened next. She wrote it during the first week of October 2010:

My hands began to tremble as I fumbled for my phone. As it was ringing, something told me it was Dr. Shaw. Two days before, I had a chat with him and Dr. Wald. They saw the bruises on my legs and questioned me at length. Then they analyzed my blood to see what it revealed.

"Marina? Dr. Shaw," he said.

"How are you?" I replied.

"I have your test results."

"You sound concerned. Am I okay?"

"Well . . . it's your white blood cell count. It's higher than we thought."

"How high?" I gulped.

"So high that it's a wonder you're alive."

Some girls I knew were gossiping not far from where I stood. I heard one say, "I know! I'd hate me, too, if I were her . . ."

"So I'm a zombie then?" I huffed.

There was an awkward pause.

"You have leukemia," he said.

The blood drained from my face.

"Wait . . . you mean," I stammered, "I have cancer? Are you sure?"

"Yes," he said. "Don't worry. We'll do everything we can."

*As tears began to cloud my eyes, I tried to take
it in. And then, as all the nearby sounds became a
muffled drone, I shuddered at the thought of being
pitied and consoled. And at the notion that my life
would never be the same.*

"I know you're scared." the doctor said.

"Who wouldn't be?" I sniffed.

"I wish that I had better news.

"Is there a cure for this?"

"We have a range of options."

"Is there one that always works?"

TO SAY MARINA was my "niece," I had to bend the truth.
Strictly speaking, she was my first cousin, once removed. But
niece seemed more befitting, and was easier to say, so this was
what I called her. Plus, it had a warmer vibe.

My bloodline to Marina has Sicilian-English roots. Our
link is on my dad's side, as her grandma is my aunt. Her mother,
Sharon, is my eldest cousin on this side, and in most ways,
the one I have the most in common with. We have the same
propensity to choose less-traveled paths and tend to think—
and see the world—in ways that are aligned. Likewise, we're
inclined to see the lighter side of things, which helps us cope
when life proceeds in problematic ways.

My grandma had a hearty laugh and loved an offbeat joke,
so I suspect our zest to jest was influenced by her. It's also a
Sicilian thing. Sicilians love to laugh. And eat, of course, and
argue with their relatives for sport. Family bonds are strong,

though—fiercely so in times of need. Loyalty and sacrifice are hardwired in the genes.

Marina was just two months old when we were introduced. It happened at a rare event in 1989—a party someone talked me into hosting at my home. I moved there shortly after my first marriage went awry and saw it as a perfect place to start my life anew. The rustic dwelling—which was in a forested locale—was quaint, uncluttered, comfortable, and easy to maintain. It also was secluded, which I viewed as opportune. The solitude that it availed was manna for my soul.

My mother called the morning of Marina's big debut. In view of rumors that my prior guests were underserved, she cautioned me about my obligations as a host.

"This time," she warned, "make sure there's toilet paper in the john. And don't serve anything that has made contact with the floor!"

She also made a point to chat with Sharon in advance, primarily to warn her of the hazards in my home. But to her credit, Sharon put my mother's fears to rest, and said that she was keen to see her daughter "melt my heart." I figured she was boasting, like new mothers often do, but sure enough, I melted like an ice cube on a grill. Marina charmed me with her coos and semblances of speech, and even seemed attuned to the vibration of my voice. The way her gaze was fixed on me got my attention too, and made me joke that she appeared to have good taste in men. But Sharon didn't buy it, nor did Mike, Marina's dad. They seemed to think that I was overrating my appeal.

My kinship with Marina had an underwhelming start. Because she lived exclusively in Georgia as a child, before her seventh birthday social calls were rare events. But once she started visiting with greater frequency, I couldn't help but notice that our stripes were much the same. I also came to see that she was wise beyond her years. Perceptive and quick-witted, too, but never to a fault. Unlike me, she wasn't prone to being indiscreet.

Our first exchange of words occurred in 1995. Marina was in Boston with her parents for the week and keen to see her kinfolk, some of whom she'd never met. On this occasion, she appeared precocious at first glance, and evidently not cut out for minding p's and q's. I watched her question everything that made a noise or moved, and be the first to stick her nose in things that looked like fun. She also seemed to see the world as generous and benign, like every oyster had a pearl, and roses had no thorns. I would have thought it strange had I not been that way once too. But never as demonstrably as she appeared to be.

In any case, I chuckled as Marina worked the room. Her appetite for fun and games appeared to have no bounds and reinforced my growing sense that we were kindred kooks. In fact, it didn't take us long to size each other up. To her, I was the uncle with a lampshade on his head. To me, she was the niece who wore her feelings on her sleeve.

A cherished photograph of us speaks volumes at a glance. Someone snapped it while we played a game of Q&A. Marina was just ten years old. The setup went like this:

"If you were broke," she asked, "what would you do?"

"How broke?" I said.

"Less dough than eggplant pizza."

"Hmm. Good question. Let me think . . ."

"Are you done yet?" She chuckled.

"What's your hurry?" I exclaimed.

She rolled her eyes and crossed her arms. I laughed and did the same. Then, before she could respond, I snatched her from her seat.

"Let go!" she shrieked.

"No chance!" I said. "Besides, you asked for this!"

With ease, I flipped her upside down, and shook her to and fro. As coins fell from her pockets to the floor, she squealed with glee.

"Help!" she screamed. "I'm being robbed!"

"And now *you're* broke!" I laughed.

"Who cares? I'm—"

"Feeling shaky?"

"No!" She giggled. "Having fun!"

At which point, I began to shake her harder. Just for fun. To her, fun was the spice of life. It figures that we clicked.

2

Enough about Me

The subtext of a story lends perspective by degrees, but if it's lacking context the allusions will be missed. In view of this, I'm forced to interrupt the narrative and offer you some insight into my proclivities. The reason I say forced is that I'm strongly disinclined. I'd rather wax my underarms with duct tape. Seriously.

Actually, I'd rather draw a picture of myself. One that would depict me in an emblematic way, but less overtly than in a discursive exposé. For instance, with a thought balloon containing question marks. And with a T-shirt on that says, "I think, therefore I *ask*."

Fittingly, a question spawned my first coherent words. As my mom prepared to read me *Horton Hears a Who*, I looked at her suspiciously and said, "Who heard a *what*?"

The questions escalated and continued through my youth. Simple, fun to ponder ones like, *Who created God?* And smart-ass ones like, *Why does Daddy yell when people yell?*

"It's *hypocwitcal*!" I'd yell.

"Don't yell!" my dad would yell.

Although my parents took my curiosity in stride, my teachers often seemed bemused or taken by surprise, like deer caught in the headlights of a fast-approaching car. It's not that I was strident, impolite, or hard to please. Nor was I contentious when their answers made no sense. My questions were the problem. They were guilelessly direct. For instance, *Why don't we have kids of color in our school?* And *Why aren't we allowed to be alone with Father Todd?* And *Why aren't wakes called rests?* And *Why do people* fight *for peace?*

As you might guess, these conversations took some awkward turns.

Librarians would call my mom. "Your son is here," they'd say. "He's reading *Gray's Anatomy*. We thought you ought to know."

I was only eight years old.

"Too young," they told my mom. "The pictures may disturb him."

"It's too late," my mom replied.

Perhaps they should have sent me to a school for misfit kids. Or humored me. Or muzzled me. Or paid me to shut up.

At any rate, what piqued me most were things that made no sense, like Santa, people dying young, the bogeyman, and girls. And people who would treat me—and my questions—with disdain. Like teachers who were too headstrong to think outside the box, or too hubristic to admit that they were at a loss.

My dad suggested that their qualms were easy to explain.

"Truth be told," he reasoned, "teachers don't get paid enough."

"To answer questions?" I inquired.

"To answer *yours*," he quipped.

In any case, I told myself, *I'm tired of striking out. I need to find another pond to fish for answers in.*

But in the end, I chose to keep my questions to myself. From where I stood, it looked as if I didn't have a choice.

Thankfully, as I became increasingly discreet, I learned to trust my instincts more and doubt my choices less. I also stopped assuming that my questions were routine, and that they would be understood or welcomed by my peers. Or that their preferences bore any likeness to my own. In contrast, I had no desire to follow any trends and few of the propensities that seemed to rule the day. Like judging or mistreating those who marched to different beats or taking pains to influence how I would be perceived. And opting to experiment with mind-distorting drugs. Or viewing alcohol as a solution to ennui.

I couldn't go along to get along. Not if I tried. But on occasion—when coerced—I would pretend to try. I even crashed a party once. I went, I saw, I left. The only thing I conquered was my fear of being seen.

Admittedly, it helped that no one noticed I was there. It also helped that I confirmed some preconceived beliefs. For instance, that my social skills were painfully inept, and that I had no business having social intercourse.

Ducks can't hang with swans, I thought. *Not if they're odd, like me. I'll share the pond, but from now on, it's with a wider berth.*

Consequently, I put up a self-protective wall—a psychic force field, if you will, to keep the swans away. I thought of it as berth control. Or an electric fence.

I did, however, keep an eye on people from afar, primarily to validate my choice to stay away. In this regard, I viewed my peers as laboratory mice. Observing their behavior gave me data to assess, enabling me to learn from their decisions and mistakes. But only from a distance, with the hazards far removed. I feared that if I got too close, their shit would hit my fan.

I also started to observe some customary themes. Like people interacting in manipulative ways or ways that were inaccurate reflections of their moods. For instance, demonstrating pride when they felt insecure or feigning nonchalance when they were desperate to be seen. Or being cold to someone they had been attracted to.

To me, it was as clear as day. I sensed it. Instantly. And yet, with few exceptions, this awareness wasn't shared. When I told others how I felt, they often questioned me, and thought that my impressions were unlikely to be true. Even those who knew me well refused to give them weight, even when what I perceived was easy to deduce.

In light of this, my answer was to practice self-restraint and to withhold the bulk of the impressions I received. Sharing them was futile and had only made things worse. All it did was give me more to question and regret.

And yet, from time to time, I couldn't help but blurt one out, and would be mystified by what occurred as a result. Like this encounter that took place when I was eight years old. It happened on a frozen pond not far from where I lived.

"Be careful on the ice," I told a boy.

"What for?" he said.

"It isn't safe. You might fall through."

He laughed and walked away.

And then I heard a thunderous crack, an uproar, and a splash. As I surmised, the boy I'd warned had fallen through the ice. I *knew* he would. I saw it happen. Clearly, in my mind.

Another time, what happened had me shaking in my Keds. I had been playing baseball on a field behind my home, and as a plane flew overhead, I had a scary thought. It was a vision of the plane *erupting into flames*.

And then, to add to my unease, an argument ensued. It was incited by a kid on the opposing team. As I recall, he wasn't fond of playing by the rules.

"Lighten up!" I shouted to the disputatious kid. "Trust me. You'll be sorry if you don't. Just wait and see! Something bad will happen!"

"What?" He laughed. "The sky will fall?"

"The only thing that's going to fall," I barked, "will be that plane! And when it happens, don't blame me! Remember, you were warned!"

To me, it was a vividly perceived presentiment. To him, it was a torrent of antagonistic bunk.

In any case, what happened next still came as a surprise. The single-engine plane began to sputter and descend. And then—as it continued to descend—the engine quit.

As flames erupted on the tail, we scattered. Hastily.

The plane crash-landed in a cloud of dust and oily smoke. My heart was thumping fiercely as it skidded to a halt, and as the cloud began to clear, I thought, *How did I know?*

The pilot was unsettled by the impact of the crash, but thankfully, did not appear to be severely hurt. And then, as I approached the plane to get a better look, it suddenly occurred to me where it had come to rest. Strangely, it was in the spot where we began our spat. In fact, in the specific spot where I forewarned the kid.

I glared at him and shook my fist. "I told you so!" I yelled. "And you thought I was crazy, right? Next time, you'll think again!"

And then I thought about my dad. *I get it now,* I mused. *I must be cursed! No wonder he gets angry when I yell!*

I shut that foolish kid up, though. He didn't say a word. And naturally, he never dared to mess with me again.

Before this happened, I downplayed impressions that proved true. They came so easily to me that I would shrug them off, or search my mind for simple ways that they could be explained. But this time, given what took place, I had to think again. I realized that my insights could no longer be dismissed.

It wasn't long before this realization was confirmed. Regarding a new insight that related to a friend, the upshot was in many ways akin to déjà vu. Or more succinctly, *préjà* vu, to coin a punny phrase.

"How's your dog today?" I asked.

"He's good," my friend replied.

"But how's his leg?"

"His leg is fine."

"But what about the fight?"

"What fight?"

"The one he had with Peter's dog. Did you forget?"

"My dog is *fine*. You must have me confused with someone else. He hasn't been in any fights or near another dog."

I shrugged and wondered if he might have had a memory lapse. I honestly believed that this was something we'd discussed.

A few days after this exchange I saw my friend again and felt compelled to ask about the status of his dog. He told me that he'd had a run-in with another dog, and that during the encounter something happened to his leg.

And then I asked him if the other dog belonged to Pete.

"Yes!" he said. "It *was* his dog. And you predicted it! Three days before it happened!"

But that makes no sense, I thought.

What did make sense was keeping my impressions to myself. The problem was that I was prone to speak before I'd think. And sure enough, when this occurred, I would be undermined. And bullied. With ferocity. And mocked. Repeatedly.

In retrospect, I was the quintessential sitting duck. Quiet, unassuming, and inherently reserved, my fragile ass was practically demanding to be kicked. And I was never one to put up any kind of fight. There was no point. "Don't poke the bears," my grandpa used to say.

My wounds were mounting quickly, though, and proving hard to heal. Bears can be relentless, I discovered, poked or not, and I was getting tired of being such an easy mark. So at the tender age of ten, I made a fateful choice. I opted to defend myself, regardless of the risk. To that end, I resolved to make myself less vulnerable, primarily by working out routinely after school. Being stronger, I deduced, would boost my confidence and act as a deterrent to my predatory peers. Otherwise, my options were to Bubble Wrap myself, pretend to be contagious, or refuse to leave the house.

At least I was creative. Desperation was my muse.

At any rate, my efforts were productive from the start. My strength increased by leaps and bounds and seemed to have no end. To boot, there was no quit in me. I was too resolute. And too perfectionistic. And afraid to stay afraid.

My persecutors were conspicuously discomposed. Most of them steered clear of me or tried to make amends, but others didn't hesitate to put me to the test. And all of them were humbled in short order. Easily. It was like swatting wingless flies. They didn't stand a chance.

Armed with newfound confidence, there was no turning back. From this point forward, exercise became my drug of choice. In fact, it's still a discipline that yields untold rewards. It keeps me sane and centered—no small task, as it turns out—and serves as a reminder that our paths are never fixed.

And that our limits can be stretched beyond what we assume.

But gyms are often crowded, loud, and hard to navigate. Picture a casino full of blowhards drenched in sweat, knocking over slot machines and screaming, "One more bet!" For focus-challenged folks—like me—gyms are akin to this. Accordingly, my preference is to exercise at home, where I can stay on task without distractions and delays. I also get to do it in the mother of home gyms. Referred to as the *dungym*—or the *heavy labor room*—I see it as a sanctum for productive self-abuse. Nonetheless, it's where I spend the best part of my day, whether it's in solitude or doling out advice.

When I was in my teens, I viewed the gym as a retreat. It was a place where I could focus solely on myself and not be sidetracked or deterred by arbitrary things. But only when I had it all—or mostly—to myself. Otherwise, I couldn't help but notice *everything*, except for things that should have been more obvious to me. Like that my fly was down, or that my shirt was inside out. Or that I had been using someone else's sweaty towel. Things I was embarrassed by but tried to underplay, in large part by pretending that I did them for effect.

To deal with situations where I didn't have an out, I found it useful to create diversions for myself. Like in the classroom, doodling as opposed to taking notes, creating farcical cartoons with convoluted themes. Or sitting near a window to stare wistfully at clouds, imagining how Rorschach might have viewed what I perceived. Anything to keep myself from being bored to tears, or jumping out a window, as I once felt called to do.

I didn't think that anyone would notice. I was wrong.

"You can't do that!" my teacher screeched.

"But I was bored!" I snapped.

Boredom was my kryptonite. It made my noggin hurt. Like anytime my parents yearned to ogle colored leaves and forced me to go with them to some godforsaken place. Of course, before departing I would beg for a reprieve, but they would fail—unfailingly—to honor my request. Instead, I had to listen to my brother's armpit farts and to my mother make a case for lactose-free cuisine.

But then she'd change the subject. "Look!" she'd say. "What pretty leaves!"

"Ooh," I'd tease. "They're red and yellow! Yay. Can we go home?"

Oddly, no one noticed that I had ADHD. Or else the conversation slipped my inattentive mind. At any rate, while I appeared to be a textbook case, the flipside was that I was often focused to a fault. But just on things that I enjoyed exploring at great length, like mysteries, absurdities, and incongruities. And any sport with objects that are kicked, propelled, or hit. Like baseball, football, and the like. In essence, sports with balls.

Looking back, my interest in athletics was a boon. When I participated in competitive events, I could express emotions that were otherwise taboo. For instance, pride, aggression, rage, and impulsivity. And since on diamonds, fields, and courts, these feelings were routine, they either went unnoticed or were frequently excused. In view of this, I could express myself more openly, with less concern about how I'd be treated or perceived.

All bets were off, however, in conventional milieus. Displays of raw emotion were less frequently excused, and far more likely to be judged, demeaned, or misconstrued. To manage this, I made myself more difficult to read, primarily by being inexpressive and aloof. I figured that if I could keep my feelings camouflaged, I wouldn't have to guard against a negative response.

The downside, though, was that it also set me more apart.

"A lot of people march to different beats," my dad explained.

"I know," I sighed, "but what if I'm required to play along?"

"Then fake it till you make it."

"It's no use."

"Don't be so sure."

"I *am*. I learned my lesson."

"Great, then tell me what you learned."

"That when in Rome, I shouldn't try to do what Romans do."

I LEARNED A different lesson with regard to speaking up. To wit, throughout my youth, when people asked for my advice, I typically responded in an inexplicit way. It was a tactic that I used to take me off the hook. I couldn't bear the thought of steering anyone astray or saying something that would be perceived as indiscreet.

But in due course—as I matured—I had a change of heart. I came to see the error of my self-protective ways and learned that I could be both empathetic and discreet. I also came to realize that my insight was a gift and that there's little value to a gift that isn't shared.

And yet, if what came into view appeared significant, I needed time to ponder it before I could respond—particularly prior to a sensitive exchange.

To buy myself some time, I'd either dance around the truth or draw attention to it in an entertaining way. I also would use humor to expose a paradox or something that appeared to contradict what I perceived. For instance, if I sensed that something wasn't ringing true, I'd say, "There's something in the room," and make a trumpet sound. It was my way of saying, "There's an elephant in here, and failing to address it isn't going to make it leave."

Recalling this reminds me of another paradox. Humor has a funny way of being serious. It calls attention to the smoke around unspoken fears, and helps us see—obliquely—that a fire may be the cause. It's laughable because it's so demonstrably absurd. We need to talk *about* the things that scare us, not *around*. Humor shines a light on things that beg to be addressed.

This may explain why humor comes so naturally to me. It's not that I have any special gift for telling jokes, or that my sense of humor has unanimous appeal. I do, however, trust myself to sense when folks are scared, and have a natural instinct to address what I perceive. I also know that problems don't get solved when they're ignored and that a dose of levity can bring them to the fore. I see it as a stealthy way of getting to the truth. It breaks defenses down so hidden fears can be revealed.

I've only scratched the surface here, but trust you get the drift. And though I'd love to tell you more—which is an outright fib—I'll spare you the particulars and give it to you straight. Essentially, I've had some life-transforming ups and downs, including some misfortunes that took years to overcome. The upshot, though, is that these things were blessings in disguise, in part because they forced me to confront my greatest fears. They set the stage for me to be Marina's ally too. As it turned out, my trials provided insight into hers and gave me the ability to speak to what ensued.

3

The Topic
of Cancer

Leukemia. Chronic myeloid. Also known as CML.

Marina's diagnosis was confirmed. Her plan was too. She'd start with chemotherapy to purge her errant cells, and have a stem cell transplant as a next—or last—resort.

Essentially, leukemia is cancer of the blood. When white blood cells are immature, or differ from the norm, they build up in the bloodstream, crowding out the healthy cells. As this takes place, immune defenses go on the decline, making it more likely that infections will occur. Other common symptoms are hot flashes and malaise, as well as weight loss, joint pain, bloating, bruising, and fatigue.

CML is caused by aberrant *myelogenous* cells, which are created solely from bone marrow in adults. *Granulocytes*— white blood cells—are what they're converted to, as well as the most common type of virus-fighting cell. Monocytes and lymphocytes are white blood cells as well, but less related to Marina's form of this disease. Moreover, chronic types—like hers—would have a slower course, whereas acute varieties occur without delay. The cure rate, though, is better. Chronic types have more unknowns.

The bottom line: the type Marina had was more complex. To find a fix would take foresight, tenacity, and luck.

But Sharon never doubted that her daughter would prevail. The same was true for Mike, Marina's wise and thoughtful dad. And yet they knew that a remission wasn't guaranteed. They also knew that paths to cures are rarely trouble-free and that there might be some she'd have to choose—and walk—alone. But now the only path she had was one she didn't choose, and one that she was forced to walk with folks she didn't know. And most of them would wear white coats and carry stethoscopes.

As Mike and Sharon steeled themselves to face the road ahead, they came to see that rest stops would be few and far between. They quickly felt the burden of Marina's growing needs and feared that meeting them would be an overwhelming task. They also found themselves reacting less to petty things, like barking dogs, slow drivers, inkless pens, and noisy kids. Compared to what was on their plate, most other problems paled.

Luckily, the Days knew how to rally to their cause. They also had some key things in their favor from the start, like access to great hospitals and systems of support. But even so, they knew that it might still not be enough. The winds of fate can be unkind and hard to redirect, despite the best-laid plans of able parents. Uncles too.

4

The Opening
Drive

Brigham and Women's Cancer Center, Boston, 7B.

I grabbed my phone to add the address to my contact list. I thought about Marina as I quickly typed it in and pictured her with grim-faced doctors speaking in hushed tones. And then I thought, *In any case, it isn't going to fly. She won't put up with this for long. And neither will her mom.*

I checked the address one more time. It was an hour away. I had intended to arrive at a specific time, but I was running late that day, like I'm inclined to do. In fact, my father jokes that I run fashionlessly late.

"You're like my doctor," he once said. "Why can't you be on time?"

"I was on time last night!" I snapped.

"By accident," he growled.

Whatever. I was late when I was born. Some things don't change.

Thankfully, the roads were clear and there were no delays. In Boston, too, the traffic flowed like Bordeaux wine in France.

Then, en route to Storrow Drive, a cabbie hit his horn.

"Moov yah cah!" I heard him shout.

"You moov yohs first!" I yelled.

I made a hostile gesture. *Why this route?* I asked myself. And then, as I sped past him, Fenway Park came into view. It made me think of baseball, and how life can throw us curves—and then, about the one my niece was gearing up to hit.

In March 2005, a curve was also thrown at me. A toxic drug reaction caused a rash of nagging ills that spurred a four-year quest to rectify my mental health.

To go this long with any type of illness takes a toll, but mood disorders come at costs that often go unseen. Symptoms can be hazy, inconsistent, and diverse, and pathways to a remedy are rarely cut and dried. To boot, depression tends to be a judgment-prone ordeal. In fact, some think it only burdens people who are weak. But people who survive it know that this is far from true. Coping with an errant mind requires deep wells of strength.

Depression is the darkest, flattest shade of black there is, and truth be told, compared to this, the blues are neon pink. Normal bouts of sadness tend to have a clear-cut cause, and aren't as all consuming, hard to manage, and prolonged. They also don't make *everything* seem absolutely bleak. Depression blunts the pleasure-sensing circuits in the brain, preventing those who have it from accessing happy thoughts. For me, this state of mind, called *anhedonia*, was the rule. Imagine being joyless, hopeless, aimless, and bereft. And that—while drowning—you're advised to ponder buoyant thoughts. This was my experience—on good days, which were few.

To be depressed for any length of time is hard to bear, but doubly so when the solutions fail to bring relief. I did survive, however. Some folks don't, so I lucked out. And once I reached the other side, I wasn't quite the same. I came to see that life was too capricious to predict and would give rise to challenges that couldn't be deterred. I also learned that fixes can be found outside the mind and that an overactive mind distorts—and masks—the truth. Perceiving this enabled me to trust my instincts more and be less prone to getting caught in ruminative loops.

Enlightening up, I called it. Taming thoughts and trusting whims. Connecting with my heart to quell the chaos in my head.

Which calls to mind another thing. This story had a twist.

As I emerged, in stages, from my melancholic haze, I witnessed the resurgence of a latent faculty. In short, my second sight became unusually acute. But not just in a fleeting or imaginary way. Instead, I was becoming more perceptive by the day.

The how and why was something that was open to debate, but trying to explain it was the least of my concerns. My challenge was to host it in a conscientious way and keep an open mind regarding how it could be used.

So short of claiming that I'm Nostradamus 2.0, let's just say I sense things that I couldn't know or guess. Not just things we all can sense—like sadness, shock, and fear—but things that are specific, like a person's place of birth. Or nicknames, hobbies, special dates, and facts about a pet. I even seem to have a knack for finding missing things. Like jewelry, wallets, keys, and heirlooms. Missing persons too.

Once I found this window to my senses was ajar, I couldn't help but lift the sash to get a better view. I now do readings and events as often as I choose, and on occasion, will appear with other psychics too. I don't, however, make predictions, promises, or claims. My purpose is to simply share whatever comes to mind, without assuming anything about what it implies.

And one last thing. For those who view soothsayers with disdain.

Besides donating my share of the proceeds from events, I offer private readings—when I'm moved to—free of charge. It makes me more accessible to those who are in need, and less attached to outcomes or the way that I'm perceived. It's also more in keeping with my sensibilities. To me, a gift that's freely shared provides the best return, especially when the purpose is to serve a higher good.

5

Room 7B

A mile before the hospital I had a funny thought. While waiting at a traffic light and fiddling with my phone, I saw a billboard with an ad displaying custom homes. It called to mind the first time that Marina came to mine, as well as her response when she caught sight of its facade.

"Holy Hogwarts!" she exclaimed. "This Muggle is agog! My uncle lives in a fictitious school of wizardry!"

We'd hired a local architect to execute the plan, but truth be told, I took the lead in crafting the design. Which might have backfired if it wasn't for my better half. Cheryl knew that I would stretch the boundaries of good taste, and that— without her guidance—I'd have stretched our budget too. Neo-Gothic fairytale is how it's been described, although to me, it calls to mind the Addams Family crib. Or Disney's Haunted Mansion, less the ectoplasmic guests.

In any case, as I recalled more of Marina's stay, my clearest memory was of our effusive late-night chats. Like me, she was a night owl and was slow to hit the sack, so while the larks were catching z's, we stayed awake and gabbed. The topics that we touched on ranged from quarks to hairy backs, and led to weighty questions, like "Was Jesus ever drunk?" Or "What disease did cured ham have?" And "Why are pants called pairs?" And "Why do courts have hearings for a person who is deaf?"

We didn't just amuse ourselves with foolish banter, though. We also talked electric cars, Nepal, and acid rain, and even shared our thoughts about what matters most in life. In fact, we even chatted once for thirteen hours straight. We would have kept on going had my wife not intervened.

☆

THERE WERE NO parking spaces when I reached the hospital, so after cursing for a spell, I looked for a valet. But by the time I tracked one down, my patience had worn thin, so in my haste, I snatched my stub and promptly dashed away.

And then I heard the valet shout, "Wait, sir! I need your keys!"

"We're good," I barked. "Just leave it there!"

"I need your keys!" he squealed.

I tossed them to him. Peevishly. Perhaps a bit too hard. And then I turned and made a beeline for the entranceway.

"Marina Day? Room 7B," the check-in person said. "The ward is in a separate wing. An aide will buzz you in."

She also should have mentioned that it might be hard to find. With less ado, I could have found Amelia Earhart's plane.

"Do you need help?" a nurse inquired.

"Depends what kind," I said.

"What are you looking for?"

"My niece."

"Her room is down the hall."

"Did she send you to find me?"

"Yes. She thought you might be lost."

"Did she describe me to you?"

"Yes. She said you'd look confused."

I frowned and acted like I took offense to her reply. When she responded ruefully, I winked and walked away.

"You're here to see Miss Day?" I heard. "Her room is over there."

I paused outside Marina's door and raised my hand to knock.

"Just go in!" a nurse exclaimed.

"She's decent, right?" I asked.

Before I dared step foot inside, I paused to clear my throat.

"Can I come in?" I shyly said.

"Depends!" Marina laughed.

"Are uncles barred?"

"Depends which one!"

"Who's *not*?"

"You had to *ask*?"

My mind searched for a comeback.

"Candygram," I finally said.

"Ha! Nice try!" Marina howled.

"I'll leave."

"You better *not*!"

Marina wore an impish grin as I came waltzing in. Relieved to see that she was clothed, I asked her for a hug.

"Ow!" she shrieked.

"Too hard?" I gulped.

"You never get my jokes!"

"I'm sorry! Did I squeeze too hard?"

"It was a *joke*," she said.

I laughed, and I hugged her mother. Sharon didn't even wince.

"See?" I said. "I'm tender!"

"As a bull," Marina jibed.

After chatting for a while to catch each other up, Marina cued me to suggest that Sharon take a break. I sensed that she could use one but was hesitant to leave.

"As long as you behave," she said.

"Forget it, then," I joked.

I had the sense to sit a prudent distance from the bed. I thought it best to stay away from any cords and tubes, and anything that I could inadvertently displace. When I was nine, I watched my grandpa have an EKG, and accidentally brushed against—and jostled off—some leads. Then when I apologized, and asked if he was mad, he laughed and said, "Don't worry, it's okay. I feel detached."

When Sharon turned her back to us, I motioned toward the door.

"Pssst," I whispered. "Let's go, kid. It's time to blow this joint!"

"Now you're talking!" she replied. "Let's make like hair and split!"

"So what you're on is helping, huh? What is it, by the way?"

"Something called Tasigna. Fingers crossed. So far, so good."

A grim-faced nurse dropped in to check Marina's vital signs. As I looked on, I yawned, and put my feet up on her bed.

"Hey!" she barked. "Your manners stink! In fact, so do your feet!"

"They do?" I said.

"Why don't you get my jokes?"

"What jokes?" I teased.

"I laugh when *you* tell jokes!" she whined. "Why don't you laugh at mine?"

"Because I'd be pretending. By the way, do *your* feet smell?"

"Are you all right? Like, in the head?"

"And does your nose run too?"

"I'll take the fifth."

"It's settled then. God made you upside down."

Marina groaned. The nurse gave her a surreptitious wink.

Our rite of trading quips and barbs seemed overplayed to some, but we were of the mind that we could never laugh enough. Humor was our native tongue in good times and in bad, and seldom failed to help us get our minds—and hearts—in sync.

And yet, our jestful jousting served another function too. For me, it was a means to feign undaunted nonchalance, especially when Marina would receive unsettling news. It also was a tactic that I used to shift her mood—and selfishly—to sidestep any disconcerting themes. Like hopelessness, uncertainty, and existential angst—matters that I had become reluctant to discuss. And for good reason, given what my recent history was. My melancholic malady had made me circumspect and loath to ponder feelings that could call it back to mind.

"Turn on your brain," Marina jibed. "Your counsel is required."

"I can't," I said.

"Why not?"

"Because my brain is off." I smirked.

"You're daft," she groaned. "And so am *I* for seeking your advice. Regardless, here's my question, should you care to prove me wrong. The drug I'm on is working, but it has some side effects. Should I be on a lower dose, or should I stay the course?"

"You're asking *me*?" I chortled. "How am *I* supposed to know?"

"Because you're psychic, dude!" She laughed. "And it's your

job to know! So be a sport, and help me out, okay? What should I do?"

"I have no clue!" I answered. "Let me think about it, though."

"What for?" she grumbled. "What's the point? Just tell me what you sense!"

"Only if you'll keep it in perspective," I replied. "Remember, all I'm getting are impressions. Nothing more."

"Except they're almost always right, so why the cautious tone?"

"But that's my point, Marina. *Often* right. Not always right."

"Often right is right enough to help, though, don't you think? Besides, when have you ever steered me wrong?"

"Deliberately?"

"As if!" She laughed. "You'd rather run an uphill marathon! Or wear a fur-lined parka to a Bikram yoga class! Or chase a pint of vodka with a quart of curdled milk!"

"Or serve as thy provider of intuitive advice?"

"Touché." She laughed. "So, are you game? Will you give it a shot?"

"I will," I said, "but just because I can't resist your charms. And only if there's rules, and you agree to all my terms."

"Whatever works for you is fine," she said. "I'm good with rules."

"Since when?" I laughed.

"I am!" she squealed. "I mean it! Ask my mom!"

"Uh-huh. Good try. You had me for a second. Maybe less."

"I thought you trusted me!" she groused. "*Whatev.* Let's hear your rules."

"The first rule is that you should trust your doctor," I

replied. "The second is that I won't tell you any scary things. The last one is that if I do, I'll have to make amends. In fact, you'll even be allowed to choose my punishment!"

"Deal!" She laughed. "I'm cruel but fair. You'll get what you deserve!"

"Go easy on me, though," I begged. "Don't be a vengeful niece!"

"Relax. We'll start off easy. Pick your piercing. Nose or tongue?"

"Do all your punishments involve some kind of puncture wound?"

Marina feigned a grimace, stilled a laugh, and flipped me off. In turn, I snapped a photograph to serve as evidence. And then I looked at her and said, "I'm having second thoughts. Regardless of how cautiously my insights are conveyed, it's possible—and likely—that you'll misinterpret them. Or lend them too much credence and do something you'll regret."

"But what, exactly, is the risk?" she said. "I'm still not clear."

"The risk is that you'll question what your doctor recommends. And in response, consider doing something indiscreet."

"You mean like squirting coffee in my anus?" She guffawed.

"You see?" I shouted. "Case in point! Have you considered this?"

"Nah." She laughed.

"Tell me the truth! I mean it! I'm concerned!"

"*The Real Housewives of Orange County* did it!" she proclaimed.

"Did what? Had coffee enemas?"

"And lived to tell the tale!"

"I still think you're Chock full o' Nuts."

"You mean cray-cray au lait?"

"Look," I groaned, "from this point on you're not allowed to think. Not until the malware is deleted from your brain."

"No need to worry," she replied. "My mom will set me straight. And so will you, I reckon, should I have misguided thoughts. Plus, I'll be receiving your intuitive advice! Unless, of course, you weasel out and fail to keep your word."

"But what about your doctor? How will he respond to this? I doubt he'll want me weighing in on what he recommends."

"Why not? He's used to people having questions and concerns!"

"But surely not when someone's psychic uncle plants the seeds. Either way, I think it's best that you don't mention me."

Marina crossed her baby blues. "Then mum's the word," she said. "I promise. I won't tell him. You can trust me. Not a peep."

"Eyes instead of fingers, huh?" I snarled. "Nice try, McFly."

"Dang!" she laughed. "I thought I'd sneak one by you! No such luck."

"I'll let it go this time," I said, "because I always do. But don't exploit my lenience, lest I view you with disdain."

And then what?"

"You may witness a vociferous tirade!"

"Just make sure you keep it clean. My mom will have your head!"

"Clean it is, then, Mrs. Clean, but first, about *your* head. Whoever scalped your lawn has cured your dandruff! Lucky you!"

"How dare you mock my hairless head? How gauche! Hast thou no shame? I figured, just this once, I'd get a break. Not this time, huh?"

"Nope. You have to earn your breaks. Besides, why should you care? A lass so fair need not have hair. You'll still be turning heads!"

"Sure, because I have no hair! But look, I have some wigs! A brown one—to look like myself—plus purple, green, and pink!"

"Purple, green, and pink?" I laughed. "Which one do you like best?"

"The purple one"—she winked—"because it goes with purple things!"

"A wig of any type is sure to flatter you," I said. "But let's get back to what you asked before we went off course. My sense is that your dose is not the issue at this point. But that's your doctor's call, okay? I'm sure he'll sort it out."

"I hope you're right," Marina said, "and that it happens soon. But since we're on the subject, do you really think he will?"

"Do ducks that are one-legged swim in circles? Take your time . . ."

"Are you a monkey's uncle? How about a simple yes!"

"Got it, boss. A simple yes. Your wish is my command. And yes, this will get handled soon. No need to rock the boat."

"Roger that," Marina said. "No need to rock the boat. Here's to smoother sailing, and I hope, to calmer seas."

Smoother sailing, calmer seas. *She'll need some luck,* I thought. *She'll also need to brace herself for swells and undertows.*

6

Marina's Love Fest

We all know social networks can connect us to our friends, but they can also be a means to serve a worthy cause. To serve Marina's cause, a Facebook page became these means. "Marina's Love Fest" was its name, and Sharon was the host. It functioned as a multipurpose notice board for friends, where notes and photos could be seen or posted any time. It also was a feed for news about Marina's health, or "Doctor-Speak for Dummies," as I labeled Sharon's posts.

About 300 people were connected to this page, which gave Marina unrestricted access to her fans. She viewed it as a meeting place for relatives and friends, but more so as her lifeline to a network of support. Additionally, besides allowing her to stay in touch, it helped her to feel less alone when she was indisposed.

Aside from this, Marina's father had his own concerns. While both his wife and daughter were in Boston or New York, Mike was home in Georgia, holding down the family fort. He also had to generate a steady income stream. Marina's treatment costs were steep, and he had little choice.

Although Mike did his best to cope with being on his own, at times, he feared the consequence of being so removed. In this regard, the love fest page was indispensable. Besides providing details when Marina's status changed, it gave him a connection to her network of support.

The page was also used to rally help at crucial times, for instance, if Marina was appearing to regress. This was set in motion first by stating her concern and then suggesting times for friends to raise a healing vibe. In theory, with us focused on the outcome she desired, healing juju would be channeled to Marina's cells. By all accounts, it seemed to work, at least to some degree. In fact, Marina often claimed that it would bring relief.

Another way the page was used was as a link to Bard. It helped Marina keep in touch with all her college friends, including the young man who had become her steady beau.

Anthony, a student, was a patient, thoughtful guy. He also was a bit like *me*, the patient part aside. In other words, tenacious, willful, curious, and droll. But even so, the nature of her illness gave him pause. He knew that it would test their bond as well as his resolve.

Because Marina's status was inclined to be in flux, Anthony was forced to make adjustments on the fly. In fact, in light of the unsettled nature of his role, I often viewed him as a knight upon an errant horse. Clearly, he was braced for what could be a scary ride, and yet the thought of jumping off—or falling—scared him more. Thankfully, Marina's fans were keen to spur him on. Their upbeat posts inspired him to be patient with the horse, and if it reared, to hold the reins with greater confidence.

7

Spring Forward, Fall Back

*T*he word was that Marina was improving every day. Strangely, though, I hadn't seen or heard from her in weeks.

Although I was relieved to hear that she was making strides, the news ran counter to my sense that trouble was afoot. Fortunately, I had access to the love fest page, where Sharon's updates—for the most part—put my mind to rest.

Marina's mind was resting too, as far as I could tell. In fact, in the beginning of November 2010, she even felt secure enough to take a class at Bard. But then in mid-December, while on campus with her friends, she started to complain about her level of fatigue.

Of course, as this persisted, we began to fear the worst.

With it appearing likely that a fix was in the cards, I wondered if the drawing board would yield a better plan. *Perhaps, I thought, a drawing board won't even be required? Maybe there's a simple fix, like homeopathy? Or kale? Or colon cleansing? Or bloodletting? Or a pet?*

Sadly, though, my wishful thoughts turned out to be for naught. A relapse was suspected and eventually confirmed.

I wondered how this would affect Marina's state of mind. Spirits break when hopes are dashed in unexpected ways, and if they break at crucial times, they might not fully mend. I know because this almost proved to be the case for me. I also know how hard it is to suffer trials alone. No one conquers spirit-crushing setbacks in a void.

The word *relapse* is such a harsh, demoralizing term. Imagine that you managed to kick cancer to the curb. And then you get the bitter news. Relapse. You're thunderstruck. It's like you weathered lightning, wiped your brow, and tripped a mine.

My mind flashed back to our last chat. Marina had been

well. To see her in good spirits was a comforting surprise. So much, in fact, that after our lighthearted tête-à-tête, I was persuaded to believe that she was on the mend. But clearly, I was ill-informed regarding this disease. Seldom is the path to beating cancer problem-free, and setbacks can be common, even during an upward trend.

CHRISTMAS WAS A week away but wasn't in the air. Marina's setback made it hard to muster any cheer. Nonetheless, I hoped it wouldn't keep her down for long. I also hoped she wouldn't spend her holiday in bed. *A Christmas Eve reprieve, I thought, would be a timely gift, and even better if it would extend to Christmas Day.* Apart from this, I hoped I'd get to see her at some point, and that if she was struggling, I could bring her some relief.

I pondered this while driving to the hospital one night—two months after my initial visit in the fall.

I need to cheer her up, I mused. *If only I knew how.*

And then I heard a Christmas song.

I'll sing to her! I thought. *"Blue Christmas" would be apropos! So would "The Worst Noel!" Or "Hark! Marina's Uncle Sings!"*

Thank God for second thoughts.

I spotted Sharon in the hall outside Marina's room. I chuckled as she staggered, yawned, and rubbed her tired eyes.

"Marina took a bathroom break," she said. "She won't be long. I'm sorry, but I have to leave. I need to get some sleep!"

I waved to Sharon as I stepped inside Marina's room. While

waiting, I felt restless, so I fiddled with my phone, and then arched crumpled pages from the *Globe* into the trash. When this began to bore me, I sat back and scanned the room. It was just one of four in this locale. They were called pods. I wondered why. To me, it made more sense to call them cells.

I pounded on the bathroom door, but there was no response.

"What's taking you so long?" I yelled. "Are you okay in there?"

I thought she might have nodded off.

"Awaken!" I exclaimed.

Alas, there was no answer.

"Hey!" I shouted. "You okay?"

Again, I pounded on the door. Again, I was ignored.

"Fear not!" I said. "I'll wait for thee. You'll find me in thy bed! Where I shall rest," I joked, "until light breaks through yonder door!"

At last I heard a clatter. Running water. Then a flush.

"Thank God," I muttered. "Now we're *both* relieved."

Still no response.

"Fine," I grumbled. "*Be* that way. Good night. I'm turning in."

I dimmed the lights, removed my shoes, and feigned a mighty yawn.

"And should you care to share thy bed," I added, "rest assured! I'll not disturb thy slumber. I'll be quiet as a mouse!"

Or quiet as a moose, I thought, *considering how I snore.* For context, think Chewbacca. With bronchitis. In a cave.

Oh well. I sighed. It was a thought. So much for that idea.

But since I lack discretion—not to mention self-restraint—I managed to ignore myself and hopped onto her bed.

And then, with mischievous delight, I pulled the covers up and waited for Marina to abandon the latrine.

When she appeared, she looked amused, albeit caught off guard. She laughed when she caught sight of me, but was too stunned to speak.

"What big eyes you have!" I said.

"The big bad wolf!" she squealed.

I kicked the covers off, jumped up, and grabbed her as she screamed. And then, as she admonished me and tried to wriggle free, a nurse appeared and noticed the condition of her sheets. They would have looked less rumpled if they had been trampled on.

"She had a restless night," I joked.

"He's *cray*!" Marina laughed.

"*C'est quoi?*" I said.

"Your Happy Meal is one fry short!" she quipped.

Marina was remorseless as I frowned at her remark. And then she turned to face the nurse and started in again.

"When he fell from the family tree," she yelled, "he hit his head!"

"No drain bramage, though," I said. "I'm just mad raving stark."

The cheerless nurse ignored us. We pretended not to care.

"I'm sorry, ma'am." Marina laughed. "He chewed through his restraints."

Again, there was no comment or reaction from the nurse. I shrugged and eyed her warily. Marina was amused.

"Nurse Ratched looks annoyed," I said, "and has a spiteful vibe. I wouldn't put it past her to put d-Con in your gruel."

"The food," Marina snickered, "is *to die for* in this place."

"And yet, they're still in business," I remarked. "Imagine that. Anyway, I'm sorry things turned out the way they did."

"Sorry is as sorry does."

"What's *that* supposed to mean?"

"I just feel so defeated. I was sure I had this licked."

"Well," I said, "you lost this round, but you could win the next."

"I'll need you in my corner, though," she said, "to cheer me on."

I paused and thought, *I'm cool with that. I'll be her corner man. I'll be her tag-team partner too, if it can be arranged.*

Regardless, her remark took me a little by surprise. I sensed that there was more to it than she was letting on, and that she had been cueing me to read between the lines. *Perhaps,* I thought, *her relapse left her feeling less assured, and counting more on my support to strengthen her resolve?* Nonetheless, I was on board, in no uncertain terms. And for the long haul, come what may. Routinely, if required.

And then I changed the subject. "Waitress, bring the check!" I quipped.

"You're treating me?" Marina laughed.

"Get out your purse," I said.

"Men," she groaned. "I knew I should have quit Mismatch. com."

"Look, I hate to meet and run, but that's below the belt!"

"Aw, my bad. Here, hug my bear. Don't worry. It's okay."

"Real men frown on PDA with cotton carnivores."

Marina crossed her arms and feigned an unconvincing pout. I smirked and said, "Your act needs work. I wasn't fooled at all. Perhaps you should have tried a fit of inauthentic rage?"

"Oh well," she laughed. "At least I tried. You can't fault me for that! But it's all good, regardless. Well, apart from seeing you."

"Hmm," I said. "It's all good, huh? Since when has this been true?"

"Strictly speaking? Not of late. In fact, I'm really scared."

"Scared is fine. Resigned is not. You've only just begun."

"I know, I'm sorry. Don't mind me. I'll live. With any luck."

"I get you're in this place," I said, "but visit, don't move in."

"You're right," she said. "I can't stay here. This place is really dark. So dark, in fact, that I'm not seeing any exit points."

"No exit points? One failed attempt, and you assume the worst?"

"I'm just afraid my luck ran out. But what do *you* foresee?"

"Well, I don't make forecasts, but I'll tell you what I think. Everyone believes that you can beat this. I do too."

"All right, what *can* you tell me, then? And don't hold back, okay?"

"When will you see Anthony?"

"Tomorrow afternoon."

"There's something that you've been afraid to ask him. Is this true?"

"It is!" she bellowed. "You're spot-on! Did you just read my mind?"

"You need to get this off your mind." I laughed. "So do it soon. You have enough to think about right now. Do you agree?"

Marina knew that Anthony was feeling out of sorts, and hoped that he'd be open to receiving some support. But when she sensed his hesitance, she started getting scared, and hoped it didn't mean that she had pressured him too much. Thankfully, the nudge I gave her seemed to help them both. It prompted them to clear the air and put them more at ease. It also made them less inclined to keep things to themselves.

THAT EVENING AT the hospital, the time passed in a flash. Before we knew it, it was shortly after 1 a.m. And yes, time flew when we had fun, but it was no excuse. The truth is that our mouths were predisposed to be ajar.

"What's your Christmas wish?" I asked as I prepared to leave.

"Hmm . . . let's see," Marina said. "I have my two front teeth. I'll have to think about it. Do you have one? Tell me yours!"

"I want you to get better, if it's not too much to ask. My other wish is not to be on Santa's naughty list."

"You might deserve to be." She laughed.

"You might be right," I groaned.

"Your first wish has potential, though."

"A better upside too."

8

In Frauds
We Trust

With 2010 behind us and the new year underway, New Englanders were fearing what appeared to be a trend. First, the Pats were ousted from the playoffs by the Jets, endangering the mental health of fans throughout the land. The other lesser matter was a sudden surge of snow. We rarely let it stop us, though. No storm's too big to brave.

And yet, it's not uncommon that a storm will slow us down. In fact, en route to Boston—three weeks into the new year—I had encountered one that should have stopped me in my tracks. But I refused to be deterred. I had to see my niece. I also was too stubborn to be stymied by a storm.

Although it took me several hours to reach the hospital, the upside was that I arrived alive, and in one piece. Instead of being grateful, though, I felt a bit dismayed. After all, heroic efforts warrant some acclaim. Not the eerie silence of a barren parking lot.

"At least Marina will be glad to see me," I affirmed.

But all she did was giggle. I was white from head to toe.

"The snowman cometh!" She guffawed.

"I'm flaking!" I exclaimed.

"Have you tried Head and Shoulders?"

"Ha! Not on this kind of snow!"

A young nurse lingered in the room, ignoring cues to leave. I pointed to the door three times. No luck. Marina grinned. I winked at her and said, "I think I hear the ice-cream truck!"

The clueless nurse appeared bemused before she left the room.

"I think we're good now, kiddo," I assured. "We lost the nurse. I see you're champing at the bit. I'm ready. Spill your beans."

Marina quickly downed some pills, and fluffed her pillow up. I had an urge to swipe it, but was able to refrain. She noticed, though, and glared at me.

"Don't even try!" she barked.

And then, keen to engage me, she began. Unflinchingly.

"When I tell people what you do," she said, "they question me. The psychic stuff I mean. Some people doubt that it's legit. But I know you, and how sincere you are about your gift. I also know that you aren't one to make misleading claims. But here's my question: Do you mind when people question you? And do you take it personally? Or try to change their mind?"

"I don't mind people having doubts." I said. "They're welcome to. It's reasonable to question things that don't make any sense. But I'm still puzzled by how well some people think I *guess*. Take the woman I met once in line at CVS. Before we talked, I had a sense that she had hurt her foot. There were no signs that this was true—like crutches or a limp—but scenes kept playing in my mind that were providing clues. The most persistent one was that she'd fallen from a horse and suffered damage to her foot when it absorbed the fall. And sure enough, when I inquired, she said that it was true. In fact, she said it happened just the way that I surmised. Of course, she also felt obliged to ask me how I guessed. Who *guesses* someone hurt their foot by falling off a horse?"

Marina shrugged and swiftly yanked the covers off her bed. Then she pointed to her feet and said, "They need some love!" It was her shameless way of asking for a foot massage. She was a touchy-feely gal who loved to be indulged, especially when she had a doting uncle to exploit. Except I never minded. I encouraged it, in fact.

"So anyway," I added, "you can ask the cynics this: How would they explain the kind of detail I provide? For instance, is it likely that I'd *guess* their date of birth? Or something like their nickname or the markings on their pet?"

"I know," she said. "The odds would have to be extremely slim. But in a way, I get it. Lots of psychics make stuff up. And most ask lots of questions, which can make them hard to trust."

"You're right," I said. "But first things first. What made you bring this up?"

"I'll tell you once I'm finished with my questions!" she exclaimed.

"Oops." I laughed. "I disremembered. You're the boss of me."

Marina had been curious about my prescient bent, but hadn't witnessed it until she was in her late teens. She asked about it after I discussed it with her mom, and was intrigued by my account of how it came to light. She'd also asked me if I had a message for a friend. I'd said, "Your friend should trust herself to do what serves her best. And as for her fiancé, he's sincere but insecure. He means well, but his sentiments are often misperceived."

Her friend's fiancé was accused of being insincere. Her friends and family were concerned that he'd betray her trust.

"Anyway," Marina sighed, "about the psychic thing...what do skeptics think—and say—when they see what you do?"

"Skeptics tend to think I make deductions," I replied. "Even when I tell them things that are outside the norm. For instance, one young man I read was clearly unimpressed. He claimed that what I told him had been easy to deduce."

"He did? What was it?"

"That his dog refused to come when called."

"For real? Why not? Did you find out?"

"His name was *Stay*," I joked.

"Stay?" she said. "You're kidding, right?"

"That's why he wouldn't come. He heard 'Come, Stay!' and got confused."

"I'm not surprised!" She laughed. "It was an oxymoron in the guise of a command! Could anything be any more confusing?"

"Tax returns?"

"Let's try this," she groaned. "From this point on, you'll act your age. And I'll reserve the right to choose the topics we discuss."

"Your proposition strikes me as one-sided," I replied. "Self-centered too. *One side fits all?* Since when? You call this fair? Anyway, regarding what we started to discuss, when I do readings and events, I don't make any claims. I just show up, let something come to mind, and spit it out. When folks ask how I do it, I'll admit that I don't know. At times, I'll share some things I've heard about what others think, but not because I'm sure it's true. It's only food for thought."

Marina looked distracted as a nurse came in the room.

"Is this guy cool?" the young nurse joked. "Should I have him removed?"

"Removed?" Marina howled. "You're kidding, right? Good luck with that!"

"A Taser might be worth a try," I joked. "Aim for my head. Don't worry. It won't hurt me. If I feel it, I'll be stunned."

Marina rolled her eyes and said, "You wouldn't even flinch!"

The nurse smiled shyly as I struck a Herculean pose.

"Relax!" Marina giggled. "He's a softy in disguise!"

"She's right," I said. "You can't judge every turtle by its shell."

We snickered as the wary nurse abruptly left the room.

"So here's the deal," I said, "about my readings and events. I get my best impressions when my gut ignores my head. Then I can relax and trust the feelings that I get. It's like when a skilled athlete reacts instinctively, or when a pilot flies a plane without familiar aids. His inner guidance system helps him choose the proper course."

"I get your drift." She chuckled. "You're on autopilot, right? But what if something goes awry? Do you direct the plane? I mean . . . there must be turbulence when you get something wrong. Do you get thrown when things don't go the way that you expect?"

"If being right is my intent, I won't be," I replied. "I have to keep my ego a safe distance from my gut. It keeps me from distorting things if nothing comes to mind. Instead, I simply say that I don't know, or I'm not sure. The truth speaks for itself, I find. It's all that matters, right?"

"Right, but *then* what do you do?" She snickered. "Juggle fruit?"

"That might be worth a try!" I laughed. "Thank you! Good thought by you. At any rate, your question jogged another memory loose. Once at one of my events, a woman was upset. She said it was because my read on her was incorrect. I chuckled, though, when she approached me after the event. She said that when I read her, what I told her was correct, but she was forced to lie to keep a secret from a friend."

"She lied?" Marina crowed. "Were you surprised, or just

relieved? And what about the skeptics? How did they react to this?"

"When doubters doubt," I said, "I let them be. Why fan the flames? Besides, to get them all on board would be like herding cats."

"Herding cats?" Marina laughed. "I'd coax them with some food. Maybe you could try this with the peeps at your events? On second thought, forget it. Skeptics never go for bribes. Especially the die-hards. They're too stubborn to be swayed. Not to mention arrogant. Why don't you set them straight?"

"Because most skeptics are fair-minded people," I explained. "They just have higher standards with regard to what they trust. At any rate, why is this subject even on your mind? Of all the things you could have asked, what made you start with this?"

"It's hard to know what's true these days," she said, "and I'm confused. That's why this stuff troubles me. I'm not sure what to trust. But what I struggle most with are the choices that I have, and how they will affect the care and status of my health. Like you, I want to have more faith in what I feel and sense, and make the right decisions, free of any major doubts. But I still have a tendency to second-guess myself. So do you ever doubt yourself, or are you always sure? How can I get better at deciding what to trust?"

"I think your brain is getting quite a workout," I replied. "But maybe you should start by asking what you can trust *most*. With things that are indefinite, I lean toward true or false. To get my drift, consider this imaginary scene.

Let's say folks around the world observe a UFO. Imagine that it's crazy big and billows purple smoke—and bears a likeness to your uncle Greg's enormous head. What is it then? Hot-air balloon? You wouldn't buy it, right? Since when are they this large, distinct, and curiously shaped? And yet, you can't assume that there are Martians at the helm. Nor can you suss that NASA launched an ill-proportioned probe."

"So don't trust anything," she said. "Don't even trust yourself."

"Well, with things like this," I said, "discretion is a must. Whenever there are variables that can't be quantified, it's hard to know with certainty what is or isn't true. In terms of where to place your bet, however, here's a tip: Compare your notes, observed and sensed, to gauge what seems *most* true, and then refine your point of view as new insights are gleaned. For things that aren't definitive, it's all that we can do."

"You may be right," Marina sighed, "but what if I feel rushed? For instance, when I have to make a choice about my care?"

"If time is of the essence," I replied, "and you're in doubt, ask someone you trust to help you make a mindful choice. But if you do and still aren't clear, you need to trust your gut. I use it like a lantern to light paths I've failed to see. Paths that lead to higher ground and more expansive views."

"So on the whole, here's what I think you mean," Marina said. "Never make assumptions. Weigh the options. Get the facts. And if I'm still not clear, enlist support or trust my gut."

"You see?" I said. "It's not *hahd* aftah all. You're wicked *smaht!*"

"I love your mother's accent! Christahphah! Go moh the lahn!"

"Or, Michael, cahl yah mutha! Is Marinah bettah yet?"

"Very funny. Wait! Don't leave! It's only 1 a.m.!"

"Hey, who said I'm leaving? I'm snowed in. I'm staying here. Unless, of course, you're going to ask more questions. Then I'll go."

"You botched your bluff!" Marina scoffed. "I saw you send that text! You just told Cheryl you might stay because of all the snow!"

"Elvis has to leave the building now, so don't be cruel."

"But wait! I have a question! Just one more before you go."

"You sure know how to push your luck. All right, but make it quick."

"I'd like to trust my hunches, but I'm scared to," she confessed. "Especially when my instincts are at odds with what I'm told. But here's my question: How do *you* know who to listen to, and what makes you give weight to what they caution you to do?"

"I see we're back to business," I replied. "You roped me in. You also asked *two* questions. I agreed to answer *one*."

"Unless you answer both of them"—she laughed—"I'll ask you *more*."

I whined that her proviso was self-serving and unfair, and that I was unwilling to comply with her request. And in short order, my response was callously dismissed.

"So here's another thing for you to think about," I said. "Imagine, for example, that while chatting with a friend, I sensed that there was something she had never told her son. For instance, that initially she planned to call him Mark, but questioned it because she had another name in mind. And what if on a whim—and unbeknownst to anyone—she changed his name from Mark to Luke right after he was born?

So how would I have known this? And what made it come to mind? But here's the kicker, should this story strike you as a stretch. Everything that I just told you actually occurred. A friend who had a son named Luke had planned to call him Mark."

"But how does this relate to my concerns?" Marina said.

"You didn't let me finish!" I exclaimed. "The point is this: You asked what I give weight to when considering advice, especially with regard to information that's perceived. That's why I shared the anecdote regarding Luke née Mark. How likely is it that what I perceived was happenstance? Or that it could have been deduced, recalled, or overheard? The odds—in case you flunked pre-algebra—are slim to none."

"Most people trust you, though," she said, "in spite of like-lihoods. Even when what you reveal is hard for them to hear."

"They trust me more when what I say is what they *hope* to hear. But you trust me completely, right?"

"Sometimes I do." She winked.

"Just sometimes?" I grumbled. "Meaning what, then? Half the time? You might do better flipping coins! Or trusting someone else!"

"I trust you even more," she chortled, "than you trust your-self! And when you can't be trusted, I ignore you. More or less."

"Perhaps you should ignore me more," I said, "and trust me less."

"Do you have any other tips you'd like me to ignore?

"Nah," I chuckled. "Just a question: Why is chili hot? Does this make sense? It's things like this that keep me up at night."

"You might try talking to yourself. You'll bore yourself to sleep."

"Was that a wisecrack or a hint? Have I been boring you?"

"Just since you arrived," she said. "Apart from that, we're good."

"Okay, boss. I get your drift. I've worn my welcome out. I'll take my leave, but don't forget the things that we discussed."

"What things? I can't remember. I ignored you."

"Like my wife."

"Ha-ha. Does she ignore you? Really?"

"Only when I speak."

9

Stool Aid

Marina's status was in flux throughout the summer months. At this point, though, eight months had passed since she'd been diagnosed. This realization gave me pause. *It's been too long,* I thought.

EN ROUTE TO see Marina, I was in a pensive mood. As it turned out, commuter traffic wasn't a concern; so absent this distraction, I could let my thoughts run free. And yet, Marina's health was still the dominating theme.

As I continued driving, Fenway Park came into view. It called to mind the first time that I viewed it from the stands as well as all the colorful sensations it aroused. I also thought about the special role I played that day. The Little League in my hometown would pass a hat at games and give what was collected to support a special cause. This time, the proceeds were to benefit the Jimmy Fund, and I was chosen to present our gift before the game. Aiding cancer research is the purpose of this fund, which the Red Sox have endorsed since 1953.

I pondered this while waiting at a light on Brookline Ave. While noticing a billboard for the fund near Fenway Park, it dawned on me that it supported people like my niece. I then recalled the many contributions I had made, despite not being able to relate to those it served. At this point, though, because the cause had a familial face, I could no longer view it in a disconnected way. It had become more real to me. More consequential too.

I parked my car and texted Sharon. "Just arrived," I said.

Without delay, she texted back. "Not soon enough," she quipped.

Sharon met me in the hall outside Marina's room. "Marina had a rotten day," she cautioned. "Brace yourself."

I did a drum roll on her door. A loud one. No response. I tried again. Still no response, so I gatecrashed the room.

Marina pouted as I gently tugged at her duvet.

"Shove over, Mrs. Cross," I said.

"I'm not amused," she groused.

"Why not?"

"For one, I can't do number two."

"No shit," I quipped.

I stilled a laugh and cleared my throat. Marina looked displeased.

"I need you to tune in!" she said.

"Tune into what?" I asked.

"You know . . ."

"Right. Your logjam."

"Dude, I mean it! Help me out!"

I welcomed any chance I had to ease Marina's pain, but only by attempting things that didn't pose a risk. Simple, gentle things, like shiatsu, Reiki, and massage, or tapping acupressure points to elevate her mood. This time, though, I had no clue about what was required. The subject wasn't one that I had thought about before.

"I'm feeling drawn right here," I said. "This spot below your ribs. I won't push hard, I promise. Just cry uncle if I do."

"Like hell!" she snapped. "I'll slug you if you hurt me!"

"Really? *Slug?*"

"It's gonna *hurt*, regardless!"

"Who?" I chuckled. "Me or you?"

As she eyed me indignantly, I cackled in her face.

"I also have a weapon!" she exclaimed.

"Pray tell?" I said.

"My pee-pee pan!"

"Your bedpan? Is it littered?"

"Seriously?"

As I pressed on her abdomen, Marina closed her eyes.

"Do you feel tender here?" I asked.

"Stop jabbing me!" she snapped.

"I'm looking for your tickle spot."

"Back off! I'll call my mom!"

And then she started groping for her bedpan. *Good,* I thought. *Her sense of humor has returned.* I braced myself to duck.

"Tell me if this hurts," I said.

"I'm dandy," she replied.

"Even if I . . ."

"Ow!"

"My bad. Too hard?"

"You couldn't tell?"

"I barely touched you, though!" I said.

"You're evil!" she exclaimed.

"But you should talk! You threatened to assault me with a pan!"

"I know, but can you blame me? You just tried to crush my spleen!"

I stuck my tongue out. She appeared impatient and annoyed.

"Your spleen is on the other side," I said.

"Right here?" she asked.

"Nope. It's slightly higher. Let me show you."

"Get away!"

Truth be told, I didn't know what drew me to this spot. I searched the room for references, or better yet, a chart. I figured there would have to be one somewhere. No such luck. So then I grabbed my phone to look it up on WebMD. And there it was. The cecum. It was right where I was drawn.

The large intestine has a pouch where it originates. This pouch is called the cecum. The appendix is attached. When blocked, it causes bouts of constipation and malaise. If partly blocked, colonics help—and laxatives as well—but larger, more impacted blocks may have to be removed.

The more I focused on this spot, the better she appeared, which gave me the impression that the outcome would be good. I couldn't stay to see, though. I was late for an event.

"Sorry, kid, I have to go," I said, "and so do you!"

"You're right," she laughed. "I hope I can. I'm ready to explode!"

"You better not. You'll make a mess. We'll have to hose you down."

"That sounds like fun, though!"

"That's the spirit!"

"I feel better now!"

"Call or text me once you drop your kids off at the pool. Before you do, though, don't forget to download *War and Peace*."

"I doubt I'll be in there that long!"

"It's been a while, correct?"

She giggled as I said good-bye and kissed her on the cheek. But not without some parting words: "Please don't explode," I said. "But if you do, don't even ask. I won't pick up your kids."

Once I hit the road again, I pondered our exchange and wondered if I should have toned the joking down a bit. When people are uneasy, laughter can provide relief, but only when encouraged in a conscientious way.

But cracking jokes is my default when I feel ill at ease, and my impulsive nature makes it hard to keep in check.

Nonetheless, I thought, *I should have tried. It's only fair. I can't presume Marina will be in a joking mood. I should have been more sensitive and let her steer the ship.*

And yet, she was a lot less agitated when I left. Recalling this was helpful. Instantly, I felt relieved.

As I exhaled, and passed the TD Garden, Sharon called.

"Marina had a big release!" she squealed.

"She did?" I said.

"Thanks to *you*!" She laughed.

"It was a crapshoot," I replied.

10

Stemming Tides

One year post-diagnosis. We had reached a tipping point. Marina's treatment options had become more circumscribed.

A stem cell transplant was Marina's next alternative. The purpose was to give her a supply of healthy cells. When transplants work, new blood-producing cells replace the old, and in the process, cancer cells are gradually destroyed.

Patients also are prescribed immune-suppressant drugs. These drugs must be continued once a transplant is received; otherwise, the donor cells aren't likely to survive.

To everyone's relief, the transplant went without a snag. Marina had a good response and didn't lose a step. Rumor also had it that she'd asked to be released.

It's rare that transplants work so fast. It came as a surprise. Not that I remember hearing anyone complain.

As I began to see her less, I kept in touch by text, and every now and then, by posting something on her page. Often it was something that I hoped would make her laugh, like "Hey! I joined a British band! It's called the Backstreet Blokes!"

I also called and left a cryptic message for her once. After saying that I had important news to share, I tried to make my voice sound like my phone was breaking up.

"I need to . . . you something, so you need to . . ." I said.

It was my way of saying *Hey, I miss you! Call me back!* But she knew me too well to fall for such a foolish trick. She called me back, but her response was equally opaque.

"You're . . . !" she said. "I . . . you! And my mom said you were . . . !"

Luckily, Marina's health continued to improve and for the next few months her life was on an even keel. She even felt secure enough to spend some time at Bard. But when she called to tell me this, I acted unaware. I figured that she wanted this to come as a surprise, so naturally, I felt obliged to act as if it did.

Although Marina's state of health continued to improve, I couldn't help but think about her previous defeats. Increasingly, I worried that the tide would start to turn. And then in February—to lend weight to my concern—Sharon intimated that red flags were being raised.

"Marina has been feeling more lethargic," Sharon said. "I just talked to her doctor. Can you call me? I'm concerned."

The upshot was that she would need another round of tests. It also meant that she would be required to leave New York and travel back to Boston where her doctor could advise. To boot, she learned that she'd be staying in room 7B. The same room—in the same cellblock—where she had stayed before.

Returning to the cancer ward is bad enough, I thought. *The least they could have done is change the setting. And the view.*

The moment she arrived, Marina called me from her room.

"I'm calling from my cell," she groused.

"Your cell phone?" I inquired.

"My jail cell!" she exclaimed. "I'm not in Kansas anymore."

While on my way to reassure Marina back in Oz, I wondered why I was in such an even-tempered mood. Given what her status was, it didn't make much sense. Regardless, I decided that the moment should be seized. So while held up in traffic, I reached underneath my seat and groped around to see if I could locate a CD. And then once I had one in hand, I did a double take. It was a disc containing songs Marina had performed. I chuckled as I slid the dusty disc into the slot, but as I listened to her voice, my mood began to change. As waves of sadness trundled in, I had to hit eject.

Marina learned to play the violin when she was young, and over time developed concert-level expertise. Eventually, she also mastered playing the guitar—as well as the piano, which came naturally to her. She also was a gifted vocalist and lyricist who liked performing—and recording—songs that she'd composed. Moreover, though she claimed to have a mediocre voice, it had a sweet, beguiling lilt that pleased this critic's ear. "Perfectly imperfect" was her modest self-critique, but my assessment was that it was heartfelt, fresh, and raw. I also found her voice to be audacious *and* demure, as if she were self-conscious but too passionate to care. To me, it made her music more emotive, pure, and real.

I was surprised to find Marina's album in my car. It was her first compendium of self-created songs, and listening to them never failed to elevate my mood. But this time, it was different. *Will she sing again?* I thought. *And will she get to dance again, or play the violin?*

Then, as I considered this, my heart began to sink. I couldn't bear the thought that my concerns were apropos, and found myself bemoaning the injustice of it all. She was so *fierce*. And gifted. And kindhearted to the core. It angered me that fate could be so indiscriminate.

I did my best to right the ship. *Put this to rest,* I thought. *No good can come from entertaining suppositious fears.*

I was resolved to keep my cart of fears behind the horse. Denying them appeared to be the way to pull it off.

I headed to Marina's room the moment I arrived. Strangely, I forgot to see the check-in personnel. Apparently, my mind was still—in large part—on my niece. This, and mulling ways to keep the horse before the cart.

But once I reached Marina's room, I felt somewhat relieved. Her smile made me anticipate receiving hopeful news.

"Hey kid," I said. "Are you okay?"

"Okay to leave," she quipped.

Sharon brought me up to speed with what was going on. Marina listened quietly and didn't seem concerned. She also claimed that she expected hiccups now and then.

"We all have bad days, right?" she said. "Less sleep, more stress, I think. Or Mercury in retrograde. The moon is full now too."

But something still seemed wrong to me. Her manner seemed contrived. I sensed that she was thinking, *I won't let myself be scared.*

"Are you all right?" I said. "Fess up."

"I'm great," Marina said.

"Then why don't I believe you? Is there something on your mind?"

"Just the same old crazy things. I'm sure I'll be okay."

"You always are in my book. What's the latest? Fill me in."

"The latest is that I've been reconsidering some things. Especially my vocation. I've been having second thoughts. To be a doctor may not be my calling after all."

"A change of heart? What prompted it?"

"I'm done with hospitals. In case you haven't noticed, being here can be a drag."

"Say no more. I get it. There's no reason to explain."

"I know, but I feel silly. I was sure, and now I'm not."

"The silly thing to do," I said, "would be to stay the course, in spite of any questions or concerns that you may have. Besides, in my opinion, you should give yourself a break. Especially given everything that you've been dealing with."

"You're right," Marina sighed. "I should be focused on my health. *Not* what I'll be doing once I beat this dreaded thing. And yet, I can't stop thinking that I need a different goal. At first I thought it would be great to tend to folks like me, but being sick for so damn long has made me think again. I'd rather do creative things that fill my heart with joy and that give people tools to live a satisfying life. Like Cheryl does. I'll be like her and write bestselling books!"

"But not *just* books." I laughed. "*Bestselling* books. That's quite a leap."

"I want my message to reach lots of people!" she exclaimed.

"Ambitious goals are great," I said, "as long as they make sense."

"What's wrong with thinking big," she huffed, "and aiming for the stars?"

"Nothing, if you don't expect to reach them right away."

"I don't mean right away!" she snapped.

"When then?"

"A future date!"

"Thank you. *Now* you make more sense."

"I do?"

"*More* sense. Not *sense*."

"I won't let you dissuade me! I'll ask Cheryl. You're no help!"

"But my advice is priceless," I retorted. "Meaning free."

"And worth your fee," she snickered.

"Hey!" I shouted. "Take it back!"

"C'mon." She laughed. "You know how much I value your advice!"

"Aw, thanks, kid," I chuckled. "You're my biggest only fan! But since you're partial to my wife, here's what she recommends: write because you *want* to, not for fortune, praise, or fame. Write because it's who you *are*, not what you want to be. And write to have a better sense of what you really think."

"Wise words, indeed," Marina said. "And yes, I *want* to write. In fact, I'm going to write about my journey. Soon, I hope!"

"I'm sure you'll do it ably and uniquely," I replied.

"And it will be to great acclaim!" she crowed. "Without a doubt!"

"*C'est sûr, Madame.*" I laughed. "*Tu as raison. Sans aucun doute!*"

Marina mentioned once before that she aspired to write, but wasn't clear about what she expected to achieve. Her tone was different this time too. It was more resolute. It made me wonder what she was attempting to convey.

Could there be more to this, I thought, *than there appears to be? And if there is, why isn't it more evident to me?*

Perhaps because it wasn't even evident to her.

In any case, her goal was more emphatically affirmed, which prompted me to make a mental note of the exchange. And then I thought to broach the subject of a joint pursuit.

"So let's write something...you and me," I said. "Once you get well. The risk, though, is that you'll be a pedantic autocrat."

"That's called projection, dude," she laughed. "*Comprenez-vous, monsieur?*"

Sharon asked about our chat the moment she returned. She had assumed that Anthony was going to be the theme.

"Did you tell Michael yet?" she asked.

"Not yet," Marina said.

"No? Why not? You said you would!"

"Chill, Mom! I'm sure he knows."

"Knows what?" I asked. "That you broke up?"

"You see?" Marina chirped.

"Really?"

"Yes, but we're still friends. I think it's for the best."

"The upside is that now you can forego deodorant. And even fail to shave your legs! I'm calling this a win."

"Very funny. Hey, does Cheryl always shave her legs?"

"Just her face. So tell me, how did Anthony respond?"

"We both were sad, and it was hard, but we should be okay. Time will heal. I only wish it would with cancer too."

"You're taking this extremely well. Much better than I thought."

"Because I have perspective now, as strange as it may sound. Compared to having cancer, breaking up is no big deal."

"True dat," I said. "But painful feelings don't discriminate."

"But when she's disappointed," Sharon said, "she plays it down. That's why I hoped she'd have a chance to process this with you."

"Your daughter would prefer to ask me questions," I replied.

"You got *that* right," Marina squawked. "I live to question you!"

"I guess I'll grin and bear it then. Forever and a day. But now I have a question. Did you get your test results? If not, then what's the holdup? Did the lab technicians quit? Or does this test involve inhaling Jell-O through a straw? If so, I think the bottleneck has been identified."

"We don't like waiting either," Sharon said, "but here's the deal. We can complain about it or accept the way it is. I'm going with the latter."

"Boo!" I joked. "Why not complain? The high road gets you kudos, but the low road gets results!"

A short time later, we became increasingly concerned. Marina's doctor said her symptoms still weren't making sense.

I took a walk with Sharon, who was keen to hear my take.

"Can you tune in?" she asked. "We're still not sure what's going on."

"I'll do my best," I said, "if you don't mind me being wrong."

"I know, don't worry. I'll be happy just to have a clue."

"Okay, then tell the staff your psychic cousin wants to help. And that they should defer to him because he has a gift."

"That will comfort them, I'm sure. All right, my lips are sealed."

"Great. It's settled. Now let's see if something comes to mind."

I told her to keep talking while I let impressions form. I find it's best to have my mind on unrelated things. Otherwise, I'm likely to get static, or a blank. The less I try, the better. Making small talk often helps.

"Well," I said, "I'll tell you what I'm getting. This is odd: I'm being drawn to something at the bottom of her spine. A cluster of rogue cells, perhaps? I'm not exactly sure. *Stray* is what comes most to mind, but that's not all I get. The cells are acting strangely. Misbehaving, in a sense."

Shortly after this, we would receive disturbing news. The lab detected cancer cells around the lumbar spine. Marina had a relapse. She had lost another round.

11

The Fault in
Her Stars

Cancer cells gone rogue. They have no sympathy or shame. Like ironhearted bullies preying on defenseless kids, they linger in the shadows, striking when your guard is down.

Marina's doctors huddled up to call another play. On third and long, with time in short supply, the stakes were high. The challenge was that all their prior plays had been in vain, which meant the only options left were drugs that weren't approved. For instance, an off-label one, if it could be procured.

Fortunately, there was one that she was cleared to use. It was an up-and-coming one called inotuzumab.

I wondered who the genius was who chose this silly name. If he'd had any sense at all, he would have called it "cure."

Regardless, inotuzumab was in a trial phase. And luckily, to our relief, Marina qualified. Her status gave her license to explore uncharted ground.

THE LOBBY AT the hospital was jammed when I arrived. All the elevators were in use at this time, too, so after waiting briefly, I proceeded to the stairs. But then, before I got there, someone yelled, "You going up?" So I thought twice and opted for an effortless ascent.

"Seven, please," I said to someone standing near the door.

"Are you a doctor?" she replied.

"No, ma'am, I'm not," I said.

"Really? Are you sure?"

"Why are you asking? Are you sick?"

"Admit it," she demanded. "You're a doctor! Am I right?"

"Okay." I shrugged. "If you insist."

"I knew it!" she exclaimed.

"I'm sorry, but I'm *not*!" I laughed. "What makes you think I am?"

"Because you look so *focused*. Like you've come to save the day!"

I smiled as I replayed this scene while ambling to the ward. *Here I come to save the day!* I thought. *Marina Day.*

I paused outside Marina's room and pounded on the door, but this time, to a rain-dance beat, Apache Nation–style.

"I knew that it was you!" Marina squealed.

"You did?" I said.

"Duh! I was expecting you!"

"To be Geronimo?"

"No," she laughed. "To visit me!"

"I think my cover's blown. Anyway, you were approved for—"

"Inotuzumab!"

"At least this time, your magic potion has a fitting name."

"You think?"

"You bet. The Mayans worshiped Inotuzumab. He was believed to be the god of life-preserving cures."

"I think you need some help," she groaned. "In fact, I'm sure of it."

"This just occurred to you?" I laughed. "Slow on the up-take, huh?"

"Right," she sighed. "Nice comeback, Patch, but let's back off the jokes. I need your help with something. I have questions. Do you mind?"

"Whatever flips your pancake, boss. I'm ready. Ask away."

My wife thought it was fitting that Marina called me Patch.

Patch Adams is a doctor who tells jokes to ailing kids. Because he uses humor to put children more at ease, Marina called me this when I reminded her of him.

"Let's be grown-ups for a change, okay?" Marina said.

"Fine," I said. "My big-boy pants are on. I'm ready. Shoot."

"Life is hit and miss," she said, "and luck is rarely earned. I mean, I was health conscious and got cancer. Fancy that. Unless I did some random thing that caused me to get sick. And what if it was something that I should have known was wrong? Could this have been avoided? What if this is all my fault?"

Marina's eyes welled up with tears, and she began to sob. I grabbed some tissues. "Thanks." She sniffed.

"These are for *me*," I joked.

Then I held her hand and let her have a good, long cry. Of course, I couldn't help but get a little teary too.

"I'm sorry, kid," I finally said. "You took me by surprise."

I tried to keep myself from choking up, to no avail. Marina waited patiently. I started in again.

"I'm sorry that you've had these kinds of questions in your head. I get it, though. It's how the mind makes sense of senseless things. Like unexpected illnesses that shake us to the core. Because we can't conceive that they can happen randomly, we look for ways to fathom and explain how they occur. Like you did when you reasoned that you made yourself get sick. But sometimes, fate sneaks up on us in unexpected ways and hands us burdens that we can't account for or avoid. Which clearly was the case for you, in spite of your concerns. Anyway, my heart reacted faster than my head. And I do jokes, not feelings. Not unless they're on my terms."

"Feelings, huh?" Marina said. "You're human? Wow. Who knew? The truth, though, is that anyone who knows you gets your shtick. Your jokes are just a smokescreen, or your way of warming up. But let's backtrack. So why do bad things happen? Rotten luck? Or do we do unconscious things to sabotage ourselves?"

"I think we're much more clueless than we even know," I said. "Which means I'm not convinced that anyone can know for sure. But here's my best as-of-this-moment theory. Drumroll, please! Some things random, others not. That's it. That's all I got."

"What a cop-out!" she exclaimed. "That's really all you got? You're crazy if you think I'll let you off the hook with *that*!"

"Well," I laughed, "I guess my mind is not so sharp today. But even so, it's wrong to think you made yourself get sick! And even if you did, so what? Who doesn't make mistakes? What do you achieve by getting angry at yourself? The present can't be changed by feeling bad about the past. I know this from experience. It only makes things worse. Besides, I thought you said that you were predisposed to this? What's the likelihood that you're in any way to blame? And what about what we found out when we looked into it? Cancer often stems from random cell-division flaws."

"But what if I woke up this gene somehow?" Marina asked. "For instance, by absorbing radiation from my phone? If I had been more careful, I might not have gotten sick!"

"I think you've lost your mind," I sighed. "Is there an app for this?"

"You mean like Find Your Mind?" she quipped.

"Or Mind Your Mind." I laughed. "But think about it. Say

you *knew* your phone could cause you harm. Would you have been more circumspect about how it was used? Without a doubt, you would have. But you didn't know for sure."

"I do my best to keep this in perspective," she replied. "But sometimes I go off the rails. Like I just did, I guess."

"Okay, so humor me," I said, "and try this on for size. Let's say you *did* wake up this gene by doing something wrong, and just to make the argument, were conscious of the risk. And let's distort the context even more to make the point. A research lab needs guinea pigs to help them with their work. They plan to do a study to find out how cancer spreads, and in a manic moment, you're inspired to volunteer. You may have jumped the gun, though. The requirements are extreme. For ninety days, you have to strap a cell phone to your head, ingest foul-smelling chemicals, and breathe polluted air. No worries, though. Since it's the norm, you'll probably survive. And if you don't, that's okay too. The upside will be *huge*."

"Upside?" she gulped. "What upside?"

"Are you serious?" I teased. "The news of your demise will be a cautionary tale!"

"But wait a sec!" Marina laughed. "I didn't *plan* to die! I wondered if I might have caused my illness by mistake!"

"You're right," I said. "Next time I speak, I'll try to make some sense."

"Nice try!" she squealed. "You can't fool me! Your tale was by design. Your purpose was to break some sort of pattern. Am I right?"

"Yes!" I said. "Except my point got lost inside my head. But now that we're on track again, imagine this *was* you. Are you at fault? You must be, right? You did a foolish thing. Except do you know everything that influenced your choice? Think before you answer. Are you sure you really know? Did you get faulty info? Were some details overlooked? Perhaps your judgment was impaired, or something slipped your mind? You might have even been insane. I'll vouch for you, okay?"

"All right, enough!" Marina snapped. "I *get* it. Maybe not. I mean . . . did I just hear you say that *I* might be insane?"

"I think we strayed off course," I said, "as we've been known to do. And yes, insane. Let's go with that. It takes you off the hook."

"Again, the pot has called the kettle black!" Marina shrieked. "Whatever. Make your stupid point. Assuming one exists."

"To recap, then," I said, "regarding what we just discussed, why would you accuse yourself of something you can't prove? And why regret mistakes that you're unlikely to have made? What if you did something you weren't even conscious of, or were misled by something that appeared to make good sense?"

"Now I'm so confused I don't know what to think," she said. "I bet that was your game plan. Get Marina all mixed up. Help her see her point is moot, since fault lines can't be proved. But even so, you must have wondered why you were depressed. So did you ever blame yourself, or suffer from regrets?"

"Ooh," I groaned. "Good question. I sure did. A lot, in fact. You know that I played football, right? In high school. College too. And did you know that football can be hazardous to heads? In fact, it's not uncommon for a blow to bruise the brain. So what if all those blows made me more apt to get depressed? We now know that concussions can have lingering effects, and that brain trauma is a lot more common than we thought. But here's the real question: Were the risks too great to take? Should I have played it safer? There's no way to know for sure. But either way, it doesn't matter if I was at fault. And it won't help for me to blame myself. Do you agree?"

"I do." she said. "And now I get it. Finally it makes sense. All those jolts and blows you suffered made you batshit nuts!"

Marina smirked and kicked her feet like kids do when they laugh. I acted hurt, and told her that she should apologize.

"I'm only kidding!" she replied. "C'mon! It's just a joke!"

"Ha!" I roared. "You fell for it again! You *always* do! Just like all those lies you tell yourself about your faults. All of us have things we wish we hadn't said or done, but feeling bad about them doesn't do us any good. We also don't have maps that show us how to plot a course. Instead, we choose most paths—or doors—without a lot of help. And sometimes we end up in rooms we're desperate to escape, wondering where the exits are when all the lights go out. But don't mistake a room that's dark for one with no way out. It's just that you might not get out the way that you got in."

"One more thing," she whispered. "A quick question. Do you mind?"

"A quick question, huh?" I laughed. "Unlike your others, right?"

"My question *will* be quick," she said. "Your answer might be long. Anyway, you've talked about how long you were depressed. At any point, were you afraid that it might never end?"

"At *every* point," I said, "although I rarely made it known. I didn't talk about it much. I feared that I'd be judged. And truth be told, I felt like people judged me all the time. It hurt—a lot—to hear things like 'You need to change your thoughts.' Or even worse, that I might need to make amends with God."

"You're kidding, right?" Marina growled. "What's wrong

with folks these days? Did they forget what Jesus said? 'Judge not, lest ye be judged!' What makes people think they know what's best for *everyone*? And what's with the assumptions? Why not wait to get the facts?

"Truth be told," she added, "people need to screen their thoughts. And hold their tongues! I don't *care* why they think that I got sick! And why would anyone point out that chemo was a risk, or that another option might have been a better choice. It doesn't help! Why can't they keep their judgments to themselves?"

"Judgments! Argggh!" I bellowed. "Those who judge . . . well, I won't judge. Okay, wait, I've changed my mind. All judgments should be judged! I know that I'm not perfect. Heck, at times I judge *myself*. In general, though, I'm smart enough to know what I don't know."

"Nice try, Patch." Marina laughed. "You know more than you know. In any case, I still don't get why people have to judge."

"I *know*!" I said. "I think we're too naïve to understand. But in the world we live in now, a lot of things are judged. Facebook posts, what someone wears, how people think and act—we judge what others do to feel less bad about ourselves. We also make assessments from a single point of view. For instance, is it always wrong to steal or tell a fib? Or might there be occasions when it can be justified? The point is that we often need more context to be clear. A judgment is a premise lacking facts and common sense."

"Wait," she said. "I sense a rant. I need to get some sleep! Proceed, but keep it short, okay? You know how you can get!"

"I don't know what you mean," I joked.

"Don't lie to me!" She huffed.

"Or what?" I scoffed. "You'll call me names?"

"Whatever," she replied.

"Whatever?" I said sharply. "Is that short for you don't care? Fine. *Whatever.* You don't care. Now where did I leave off?"

"Leave off?" she barked. "You're kidding, right? I had to shut you up!"

"As I recall," I muttered, "you advised me to proceed."

Marina sighed. "Then be my guest. Good night. I need to sleep."

"You can't," I said. "It's impolite. But who am I to judge? Regardless, you can't blame me, right? I'm human, so I judge. And anytime you blame, you judge, which makes you guilty too."

"You're nucking futs," Marina groaned. "Can I ignore you now?"

"I think you mean ignore me more than usual," I quipped. "At any rate, to wrap this up, most judgments are affronts— unreasonable assumptions based on biased points of view. They form when people fear positions other than their own, and feel compelled to challenge those their tribe views as a threat. But why are tribal mind-sets still so common in our world? It's been a while since caves were homes, so why do they persist? Perhaps because we still have trouble trusting other tribes. We feel less vulnerable with those who share our core beliefs. They reinforce the notion that we're on the side of truth."

"Thanks for your judgmental food for thought." Marina yawned. "You saved me from a restless night by boring me to sleep."

12

Tell Me All
Your Thoughts
on God

To see Marina faring well again was a relief. Since inotuzumab had not been FDA approved, no one had a sense of how—or if—she would respond. But given that for several months there was an upward trend, I couldn't help but wonder if she'd stumbled on her fix.

But then, in August 2012, the tide turned once again.

To our dismay, familiar symptoms slowly reared their heads. Sleep was hard to come by, too, which had us all concerned. *This is discomforting,* I thought. *What if this trend persists?*

Marina also found herself with several new concerns. The first one was a palsy on the left side of her face. Her most apparent symptoms—other than a droopy mouth—were slurry speech, a lazy eyelid, and a swollen jaw.

Imagine waking up to this. It's pretty scary stuff. To top it off, it spelled the end of inotuzumab.

This setback scared me more than those that she'd sustained before, owing largely to its more conspicuous result. I also was concerned about the toll that it would take. My biggest fear was that she'd view it as the final straw.

Feigning nonchalance was never something I did well, but this time, for Marina's sake, I felt obliged to try.

"Why are you still here?" I joked. "Don't tell me it's the food. Regardless, I'm surprised. I thought this place gave you the creeps!"

"It does." She laughed. "This place and *you.* Two things I can't escape."

"I see you're in a joking mood. What's with the twisted grin?"

"You noticed, huh? You're good that way. I'm sure I'm quite a sight."

"When Elvis snarled, his fans would swoon. I'm sure your fans will, too."

"I'm nothin' but a hound dog, though."

"You're beautiful to me."

"Then you should get your eyes checked. Or be honest. Take your pick."

"My eyes are fine, unless my wife moves something in the fridge. So what's the scoop about the droop? It must have been a shock!"

"The doctor said it's likely to resolve itself in time. Meanwhile, I'm resigned to scaring children with my face."

"It looks just like it always has! Except the bottom part."

"I fail to see the humor," she replied.

"You will," I teased. "Hold on, I'll get a mirror."

"That's not funny!"

"Lighten up!"

"Not until you tell me that you're sorry!" she exclaimed.

"Fine," I said. "I'm sorry that you didn't get the joke. And sorry that this happened. But take heart. This too shall pass."

"So they say," she sighed, "although with *my* luck, maybe not."

"Your attitude concerns me. But I get it. You're upset."

"Of course I am!" Marina squealed. "Who wouldn't be? *Whatev.* I'd like to change the subject. I've been working on a piece. I'll play it for you now, okay? I think you'll be impressed."

The arrangement she composed was for a course she'd had at Bard. Her task was to create a rhythmic piece from random sounds, like those that she'd routinely hear both in and near her room. For instance, noises from machines that tracked her vital signs. The sounds of nurses chatting and performing routine tasks. The clack-clack-clack of footsteps on the tile outside her suite. Doors that opened, drawers that closed. Her heartbeat . . . beep, beep, beep.

As I was listening to the piece, a lump formed in my throat. I thought of all the sleepless nights I'd suffered while depressed, and how the background noises had the flavor of a dirge. It saddened me to think she could perceive them this way, too, these sounds a grim reminder that her life was on the ropes.

"I thought I'd beat this thing," she said, "once all was said and done. I also thought that being here gave me a better chance. But clearly I was wrong to think my fate could be controlled. If stuff is meant to happen, there's not much that we can do."

"We influence our fate," I said, "but can it be controlled? What would be the protocol? Is this a valid goal? To cite all possibilities would be the place to start, except it isn't possible, and situations change. They also change in ways we can't prepare for or predict."

"I know," Marina grumbled, "but this fight was never fair. I thought I had more say about my outcome than I did. It makes me wonder what I may have missed that would have helped. For instance, can a person, place, or thing affect our fate? Have I been blind to things like this? Could this be why I've failed?"

"Failed?" I said. "You're still here, right? You were last time I checked! If what you mean is failed *thus far*, okay, but is it true? Your so-called failures might prove instrumental to your cure! But since you asked me, yes, connections do affect our fate. In fact, we're *all* connected. We do nothing in a void. Everything we do has repercussions, big and small. And what about entanglement? Are you aware of this? Objects that are parted will behave as if they're not. It looks like spooky action at a distance, Einstein said. I bet he would have probed this more, if he had time and space. Time is relative, he said, and space is in our head. Also, space ain't really space, and time may not exist. What we think is real may be a figment of our mind."

Marina yawned, and closed her eyes. It seemed she needed rest. I asked, but she sat up and said, "We've only just begun!"

And then she had more questions.

"Where is God in all of this? By the way, what *are* your thoughts on God? Does he exist?"

"It's fine to talk about a higher power," I replied. "But why give it a gender? And why must it have a beard? And why do we perceive it as demanding and austere?"

"I often ask myself these questions too," Marina said.

"I also wonder why we think God judges us," I said. "And why we think eternal life is something to be earned."

"I think *I'll* make the cut," she quipped, "but *you* don't have a chance."

"I beg to differ," I replied. "God loves me. I'm a lock. I'm going to the Cosmic Club of Everlasting Souls!"

"The Cosmic Club of Everlasting Souls?" Marina laughed. "That's what you're calling heaven, right? Is heaven even real?"

"No one really knows what happens when we die," I said. "I've heard some lovely anecdotes and read some hopeful things, but none have changed my point of view enough to be convinced. I bet this comes as a surprise. I talk to dead folks, right? So how can I have doubts about what happens when we die? I guess I'm still not clear enough about how all this works. I don't just mean how things go down when people leave this world. I mean—"

"How things go *down*?" she snapped.

I paused. "Poor choice of words?"

"The Cosmic Club is *up*," she laughed. "At least that's what I've heard."

"The Mile-High Club is too," I joked.

"I wouldn't know," she said.

"Nor would I!" I emphasized. "But let's get back on point. Some folks doubt departed souls communicate with me, and think I'm gleaning info from their loved ones in the flesh. But what if I know something that no one was ever told? For instance, 'Auntie's ring is in a trunk in the garage.' And what if someone checks, and is surprised to find it there? Whose mind would I have read if he or she was not aware?"

"I know, you're right," Marina said. "What would they say to *that*? It makes me wonder what religious people think of you. Or psychic things, in general. Does it make them ill at ease? I bet some people figure evil spirits are involved. It's funny, though, that there are those who question what you do, but never question things about their faith that don't make sense."

"That's because they fear the consequences," I replied. "When people drink the Kool-Aid and believe it came from God, they rarely dare to question why it tastes like dirty socks. And then we wonder why it makes them do ungodly things."

"It shouldn't be taboo to question things," Marina sighed. "And what's with the *commandments*? Shouldn't they be *moral codes*? And why is it a virtue to buy everything we're told, regardless of the context? Or the kind of sense it makes?"

"Because," I said, "dogmatic preachers want us to be sheep. Mindless, docile sheep, that is, who won't stray from the herd. Willful sheep are more inclined to wander from the pen, so in effect, the blind-faith thing is meant to pen us in. If it's seen as a virtue, we won't look outside the fence. But I can't help but look, and when I do, I question things. For instance, why are questions bad, and why is blind faith good? The answer that I get is almost always something rote, like common quotes from scripture, or a tale from some old text. In fact, in many cases, the discussion goes like this:

"'Why blind faith?' I ask.

"'See Matthew 14:31.'

"'Do you trust everything you read?'

"'I trust the word of God.'

"'Are you convinced that it's his word?'

"'The Bible *says* it is.'

"So basically," I added, "here's my take on this exchange: a God we need blind faith to trust demands that faith be blind."

"So having faith is fine," Marina said, "but don't make leaps."

"In large part, yes," I answered. "No one's mind should be this closed! How likely is it that one faith—or text—is absolute? And don't you think it's likely that these documents have flaws? Contextual gaffes? Translation goofs? Some *e*'s that look like *g*'s? Either way, we know that they were altered and misused. What's the likelihood that parts weren't added, lost, or changed? Or that the authors didn't misinterpret what they heard?"

"You're right," she said. "I'm sure they had diverse perspectives too. Nonetheless, I doubt that any text is error-free. Nor do I believe that they aren't biased in some way."

"Here's a case in point," I said, "that makes the problem clear. Let's say your holy handbook says you can't eat meat today. By the way, is chicken meat? And what's with fish and pork? Pork's the other white meat, right? I'm sorry. I digressed. But really, what if leaders of your faith amend this rule? For instance, say the pope decides to lift constraints on meat? Is God alerted via text? Or does he simply *know*? Say carnivorous sins occur *before* meat sanctions pass, or someone croaks before they beg forgiveness? What's the deal? Are they at fault for what they did before the rule was changed? And would they have to do a stiffer penance? Is that fair? I don't propose these questions to dissuade you from your faith. I'm just sincerely asking if it *all* makes perfect sense? If you weren't scared what God would think, how would you answer this?"

"Carnivorous sins?" Marina laughed. "So what's the outcome? Hell? For kittens too? They're carnivores! Do they get docked for this? Can they eat mice on Friday? If they do, is it a sin?"

"Animals get passes, kid." I laughed. "Especially cats. But jokes aside, would having questions jeopardize your faith? Why not take the parts you like and disregard the rest? Why do people care so much about what others think? This with-us-or-against us thing is wrong. It *never* works. And scaring people won't inspire a solid, heartfelt faith. All it does is brainwash folks and turn them into sheep."

"I think it's wrong to disrespect a faith," Marina said. "People need to have more tolerance for other views. Don't they see they're doing what they don't want done to them? Why can't people get along? It's childish, don't you think?"

"It shows," I said, "that human beings think in human

terms. And human terms are, as a rule, parochial and fixed. People are afraid to look outside their tribal lines. Instead, they yearn for certainty and guard against their fears. So once they do the download on a set of strict beliefs, if something contradicts them, it goes hard against their grain. It wobbles their foundation and disturbs their solid ground. And shaky ground can't hold the roots of shaky paradigms."

"The more things shake, the more there is at stake," Marina mused.

"Yes," I said, "and people raise the ante on their bets. It makes them dig in deeper and take even firmer stands. But why can't they back off and keep their leanings to themselves? What's the point of hating those with different views of God? It's shameful that intolerance is fostered in some faiths. If you're not in, you're clearly *out*. There is no middle ground."

Marina looked reflective as she scanned the moonlit sky. I figured she was pondering the questions we discussed, and maybe even asking why we ventured down this road. And then, when dinner came, I asked a nurse to bring some wine. Marina rolled her eyes and flicked a green bean off her plate. It sparked a brief but lively fight involving food in flight.

"So what was on our minds?" she laughed. "Before our battle raged?"

"Regarding views on God," I said, "what's wrong with different slants? And why not reconsider things that don't make any sense? Are we afraid the Cosmic Club won't let us in the door? Wouldn't an all-loving God cut us a little slack? If not, God has an ego, right? A monstrous one at that."

"It's hard to move past old ideas of right and wrong," she said. "To do so, we must challenge those who want us to conform. Because to them, ironically, the strongest don't survive. Those who are strong minded don't get in the Cosmic Club!"

"We move past Santa, right?" I laughed. "The Easter Bunny too. We might not, though, if our misgivings landed us in hell."

"I know," Marina groaned. "It's clear that fear still runs the show. We're taught that we'll be punished if we question what we're told."

"The ways we're taught to think of God," I said, "still trip us up. We view him as a cosmic dad enforcing earthly chores—or an ill-tempered, spiteful king who judges from the sky. Betray him or ignore his rules, and you'll have hell to pay. Buy this, even slightly, and you'll always live in fear. You won't forget the consequence of messing something up! You'll burn in hell, forever. That's a bit excessive, right?"

"Relax." Marina laughed. "Our souls are fleshless. No one burns. I get your quarrel, though, regarding rigid points of view. I even know some atheists that can be like this too. I think it's just as wrong to say that God cannot exist."

"So why not be agnostic then," I asked, "if you're not sure? Why all out, if not all in? Why have a narrow mind? Why would things be only right and wrong, or black and white? Why don't folks of different faiths look for some common ground? And why is hell the price we pay for questioning some things? Or even just misjudging what we read or what we're told?"

"And what if we repent," she mused, "but really aren't contrite? Are we excused by simply owning up to our mistakes?"

"Right!" I said. "And what if we're contrite, but don't repent? Does lying serve us better than neglecting to atone?

What if we don't know we sinned? Does God consider this? I only hope Saint Peter goes for bribes and shameless pleas. If not, then heaven help us. We won't have a snowball's chance. Can you imagine Judgment Day? It's apt to go like this: 'Michael, you kicked ass down there. Your mom called you a saint. But you were prone to question things. Enjoy your stay in hell.'"

"I can see why that would fire you up." Marina laughed. "I do get what you mean, though. It's okay to question things! And by the way, my view of God is as a higher source. I also don't feel bound to any single faith or creed. But what's your take on all of this? Is there a way you lean?"

"My faith is modest, circumspect, and doctrineless," I said. "I call it silentology. I keep it to myself. Open-minded inquisition is the paradigm. There are no mandates, biases, or rigid set of rules. The truth is not dictated or defined in just one way, and God is not a prickly king who favors servile fans. I also doubt that joining any fan club gives me perks. To think God has an ego is absurd to say the least. This doesn't mean I view historic VIPs as frauds. In fact, some may have been evolved to noteworthy extents. Significant, but not in ways that we can comprehend. Close to God, I'll even say, if God is viewed as truth. With higher consciousness as well. Who knows? And *that's* my point."

13

Gray Matters

Another stem cell transplant was Marina's next resort. Without much knowledge of the risks, I viewed this as good news. Because her first infusion had a measure of success, I figured it was worth a shot to go this route again.

But first she needed donor cells that were compatible. To this end—given that they had to be located first—Marina's second transplant was delayed for several weeks.

The upshot was that to avoid the doldrums during her wait, she chose to do it in a place where this could be ensured. Specifically, aboard my parents' waterborne hotel—the good ship *Aphrodite*—where a room had been reserved.

Of course, my parents had concerns about Marina's care. They also hoped a setback wouldn't make her miss the trip. To their relief, however, she felt well enough to go and had an uneventful—if not perfect—stretch of days.

Marina felt unfettered as she toured Maine's southern coast, and even left the boat to spend a little time alone. Otherwise, she rested and was pampered by the crew, all of whom were happy to accommodate her needs.

Although I couldn't make the trip, Marina kept in touch and humored me with wisecracks like "I'm glad that you're not here." And while she wasn't up to doing waterskiing stunts, it was enough for her to see the ocean with her mom. She always relished the allure and grandeur of the sea. To smell and breathe the salt sea air was comforting to her, and as the waves lulled her to sleep, she loved the tranquil vibe.

While on my way to see her—just before her cells were due—I thought about her journey and its problematic trend. The ups were short, the downs were long, and hopes were often dashed. And now she had to steel herself to go another round. It made me wonder what it felt like to be in her shoes.

Fortuitously, I recalled a phrase that helped me once: you'll know how strong you are when it's the only choice you have.

☆

THE STAFF APPEARED aloof as I approached Marina's room. Recalling that I'd had the same impression once before, I thought it might be fun to see if I could stir them up.

"I'm here for my exam," I said. "There's something in my nose. It's either mucus, glue, or gum. Can someone take a look?"

"Excuse me, sir," a nurse replied. "Can you say that again?"

"You didn't hear me, did you? You remind me of my wife! I'm here to see Marina. Don't get up. I know the way."

I sauntered to Marina's room and pounded on the door. This time, to the beat of "We Will Rock You." Classic Queen.

"What's up, Doc?" I chortled as I flopped onto her bed.

"Not much, Bugs," Marina said. "I'm still here, doing time. Chillin' till my cells arrive, which should be fairly soon."

"Where does one get stem cells from?" I asked. "A stem cell bank?"

"Yes," she said, "to locate cells that are a proper match. But even if they are, it won't ensure a good result. The cells still have to hit it off with all my other cells. I'll need immune-suppressants too. I don't have any choice."

"For any transplant, I assume. Just like the first time, right? Will you keep taking what you're on, or switch to something else?"

"The only thing I care about right now is that it works. I also hope it's worth the risk. Do you have any thoughts?"

"Your doctor has good judgment, right? So why are you concerned?"

"I know. You're right. I'm just afraid that something will go wrong. And say it does? What will I do? Curl up and wait to die?"

"Don't be such a baby. There are much worse things than death. Okay, I just said that because . . . I can't control my mouth. Actually, I'm trying to ignore what you just said!"

"It's just the place I go," she sighed, "whenever I get scared."

"It sounds like existential dread," I said. "I know it well."

"Do you believe that this is all there is?" Marina asked. "And are there really other planes—or realms—where life exists? I wish there was an easy way for us to know for sure. Do you have any thoughts about what happens when we die?"

"From what I've seen, we're thrown in holes and covered up with dirt."

"Thank you for the pleasant thought. Sometimes you're such a dope!"

"In my defense, I could have said we go to hell and burn."

"Your six-pack is a few beers short!" She laughed. "Like, four or five. In any case, what do you think? Do we survive our death?"

"No one knows for sure," I said, "that there's an afterlife, but if there's not, the upside is that we'll be unaware. But since you clearly don't intend to let me off the hook, I'll give you my best guess—in view of all I've seen and heard. I think that there is more to all of us than meets the eye, and that—in some way, shape, or form—a part of us survives. Basically, we're energy, which cannot be destroyed. It can change form, however, which is fun to contemplate. Because if we can choose our form, I'm coming back as God. And then I'll make you like my jokes. Of course, I'll cure you first."

"You're awesome, dude," Marina laughed. "So selfless! And disturbed. But even so, I think you might on to something here. A skeptic might not think so, but I bet freethinkers would."

"Skeptics see things through the lens of science," I replied. "But even skeptics know that modern science has its flaws and that there still are things it can't account for or disprove. It bothers me when skeptics rule things out that are unknown. It's fine to say they seem far-fetched, or hard to comprehend, or even that you need to have more proof to be convinced. But how can anyone be *sure* that something can't exist? Before the ancient Greeks weighed in, who knew the Earth was round? And who would have predicted that we'd travel in winged tubes, or access information with a small handheld device? In twenty years, we'll have these things implanted in our heads!"

"Anyway," Marina chuckled, "where did we leave off?"

"We were discussing life and death," I said.

"That's right." She laughed. "I'd like to trust that life goes on, but here's what rocks my faith: the folks who don't believe it make more sense than those who do. Folks like Stephen Hawking. He'd be hard to argue with."

"Why would you then?" I said. "What would you win if you were right? But either way, I would enjoy exploring this with him, and maybe even sharing my unscientific view. Or, for fun, I could decide to do my psychic thing. If I tuned into something he was sure I didn't know, how would he account for this? A trick? A lucky guess? Imagine that I sensed he had a scar on his left foot, and linked it to a mishap that occurred when he was six? How would he explain this? Would he think that I'd been told? And if it couldn't be explained, what else might he not know?"

"You're right," she said. "I can't imagine how he would respond. I doubt that he'd be swayed, though."

"No? Why not?"

"Because he's smart."

"But so am I!"

"You're *sorta* smart."

"Don't you mean *strangely* smart?"

"Yes." Marina laughed. "It's strange that you are ever smart."

"Anyway," I groaned, "here's where I go with all this stuff. The universe. Where does it end, and what's *outside* this point? Physicists have theories that are surely worth a look. But something formed from nothing? Who could ever fathom this? I'm not the brightest bulb on any tree, but I sure can't. Theories give us insight into what might have occurred, but who can fathom *nothing*, or how life came from a void? To think that minds can stretch enough to grasp this is a stretch. And yes, that was indeed a pun. Did you just fall asleep?"

"I'm *not* asleep!" Marina squealed. "I only closed my eyes! I tried to think of something formed from nothing! Like you said!"

"Did you have any luck?" I asked. "If so, I'll get a nurse. But we're *all* mysteries, aren't we? Think about how we evolved! We went from grunts and whimpers to defining thoughts with words. And think about where thoughts come from. It's trippy, don't you think? The answer is a wrinkly, three-pound blob of grayish mush! But if your mind still isn't blown, here's something else to mull: Before there was a universe, did anything exist? And could there have been nothing? What is nothing? What's it like?"

"Let's x-ray your head"—she laughed—"and maybe then we'll see."

"Take it back," I grumbled, "or I'll call the niece police! Before I do, though, let's address these questions. Are you game?"

"If you say so." Marina shrugged. "As if I have a choice."

"Let's imagine there was once no universe at all. And then it happened. Bang! *Big* bang, I mean. And God was pleased. So when, and how, did this take place? And why? Was God forlorn? Was he depressed, upset, or bored without life forms to judge? It's just another question we can't answer. Well, *I* can't."

"You mentioned theories, though," she said. "Have any been confirmed?"

"We're closing in on one," I said. "Higgs boson. Ring a bell?"

"Vaguely. Yes."

"So clearly, no."

"You mean that God thing, right?"

"I think you mean God particle."

"I do? I mean, I *do*!"

"You're lying to a psychic, kid. Don't waste your time. Or mine."

"All right," she grumbled. "I'll play dumb. God *what*? Enlighten me."

"It may explain," I said, "how mass and matter came to be!"

"For real?" she said. "Say more about this, then. I want to know!"

"A giant tunnel has been built in Switzerland," I said. "But not just any tunnel. This one is a giant ring. Anyway, it forms the core of a unique machine. The Large Hadron Collider. Have you heard of it before? It's used to study subatomic particles in depth. These particles are *hadrons*, from the word for *thick* in Greek. When they collide, they break into a lot of smaller parts, providing quantum data that may redefine our world. For instance, if it works, the big bang theory could prove true, and we might find dimensions other than the ones we know."

"You're sounding like a science geek," she said. "At least to me. Regardless, now I'd like to know what made you bring this up."

"To show that we can't close our eyes to things we can't conceive."

"Then how can scientists rule out an afterlife?" she asked.

"Some do," I said, "because what they call proof is so concrete. But how would they account for all the things we can't explain? Like kids recalling former lives in tongues they've never heard, or mediums who know odd things about loved ones who've passed. I don't mean things that can be guessed, like 'Mary was complex,' but rather, things like 'Fred's birthmark was shaped like Idaho.'"

"Dude!" she said. "Did someone ever drop you on your head? I think I get your drift, though. Elephants are in the room. And skeptics fail to see them or admit that they exist."

"It seems," I said, "that we see *lots* of elephants these days. Incidentally, guess how much they weigh? A lot, you say? Well how does *three tons* grab you? Some are *twice* that size, I've heard! In fact, they—"

"Focus, dude!" She laughed.

"On what?" I said.

"Your point!"

"Indeed," I said. "So if the big bang theory can be proved, what kinds of other insights might be possible in time? And then who knows how this will change the way we look at things? Perhaps we'll even start to witness things we can't conceive. Like life on other planets. Or an honest bureaucrat. The notion of an afterlife may seem unlikely, too, and yet, the day may come when we won't question it at all."

"Do you believe that we'll encounter life from different worlds?"

"We have already!" I replied. "You've seen the tabloids, right? Apparently, abductions are a fairly common thing."

"You were abducted, right?" she teased. "That would explain a lot!"

"Many years ago," I joked, "by Martian fishermen. But I lucked out. They threw me back."

"You must have been too small."

"Or flavorless."

"What happened then?"

"My story was rebuked."

"The other fish pooh-poohed it, huh?"

"They thought I made it up."

"Because the pond was all they knew."

"Exactly. Case in point."

IT WAS RAINING hard that night as I was driving home. While pondering Marina and the topics we discussed, I smiled, recalling all the times we chose less-traveled paths. We never second-guessed them, though, no matter where they led. They always gave us something fun to question and assess.

As I got on the freeway, I could barely see the road. And then Marina called. I tapped the home screen on my phone.

"Are you okay?" she asked. "I heard the rain and was concerned."

"I'm fine," I said. "Just finished helping Noah load the ark."

"I also called to thank you for the chat we had tonight. I'm grateful that you talk to me in such a normal way."

"Normal? Are you crazy?"

"What I mean is . . . you're *yourself*. You let me bring up things that people can't—or won't—discuss, and never walk on eggshells, or behave as if I'm frail. You're just the way you *always* are. Your same old goofy self!"

"And it takes one to know one, right? But thank you for the props. Truth be told, I think it's you who should get all the praise. I can always be myself because you're always *you*."

"How are the roads?" Marina asked. "This rain is crazy, right?"

"Hold on," I said. "I can't see shit. Oh no! I almost . . . whew!"

"Very funny. Maybe I should let you watch the road?"

"I'll text you once I'm home, okay? Now, try to get some sleep!"

"Okay, I will. I love you. Please be safe."

"I love you *more*!"

"That's what you say to Cheryl!"

"Yes, to her, my mom, and you."

"Wow! I'm in good company! Be careful now. Good night!"

"Will do, boss. There's less rain now. No need to be concerned. Call me once you have a transplant date. I'm standing by."

14

Waiting
for Lars

November was a consequential month in 2012. Burma had an earthquake. Guatemala had one too. A marathon was canceled. And Marina met her match.

Transplant day. So eagerly awaited. Questioned too.

While driving to the hospital—with Cheryl in the car—I fielded her complaints and thought, *At least I'm not alone.* And yet, despite her company, I still felt ill at ease.

At first, I figured it was best to keep this to myself, but as we passed the Zakim Bridge, it all came spilling out.

"I hope I'm wrong," I said, "but I don't like the way I feel."

"What's the problem?" Cheryl asked.

"The transplant. I'm concerned."

"What are you concerned about?"

"The outcome."

"*This* is new."

"I thought it might upset you, so I kept it to myself. Chances are, it's just me thinking scary things again."

"Relax, okay? Marina will be fine. She's in good hands. Besides, who knows? Perhaps your gut is just more scared than right?"

We made good time and reached the hospital at 5 p.m. Thanks to Cheryl, we were prompt and missed the rush-hour jams.

As we approached the entrance, I was feigning nonchalance.

"Reveal your status." Cheryl urged.

"Collected." I replied.

"You don't appear to be," She laughed.

"That's it. We're going home."

"Ha-ha. Too late. Don't worry, though."

"Why not?"

"I've got your back!"

"But what about my front?"

"All sides are covered. You'll be *fine*."

"If not, I'll just pretend to be."

"Like you just did? Good luck!"

Mike and Sharon greeted us outside Marina's room. On the surface, they seemed optimistic and assured. Marina seemed untroubled, too, which put me more at ease. If she had any fears, no one could tell. Not even me.

"Where's your donor from?" I asked.

"Asgard," Marina joked.

"You mean the land of Nordic gods?"

"I mean from Nordic stock!"

She didn't know her donor's name, but chose to call him Lars. I grinned when she described him as her picture-perfect match.

"He's six feet two with eyes of blue," she gushed. "Puts you to shame. An awe-inspiring specimen with superhuman genes! And once these cells become my own, I'll have prodigious strength! Marina the almighty! Superhuman, thanks to Lars!"

It pleased me that her flight of fancy had a cheeky vibe. *If affirmations work,* I thought, *this is the way to go.*

A nurse came in and said that Lars was going to be delayed.

"Lars is late for your big date?" I joked. "And you're surprised? I mean, he *is* a god correct? You'll make concessions, right?"

Lars arrived an hour late. No reason, kiss, or rose. A nurse came strolling in with him, and plopped him on a shelf.

That's it? I thought. *No drumroll, horn, parade, or marching band?* It seemed so wrong. Marina's life depended on that bag!

"Marina . . . is this him?" I asked. "I think we better check.

Some guy—Bruce something—once received a tainted batch of cells."

"Then what?" she groaned.

"He pitched a fit, turned green, and split his pants!"

Mike and Sharon looked amused. Marina rolled her eyes. Cheryl frowned and shook her head. "I *married* him?" she quipped.

On strips of inch-wide paper, Sharon scribbled healing words. Things like "I accept this gift of life and vibrant health," and "With these cells, my body thrives, and I am free to heal." Then she put the strips together with the bag of cells and hung them on a tall steel rack placed near Marina's bed.

I stood to get a closer look at what was in the bag. Compared to her first transplant, something looked a bit askew. The contents had a slightly darker hue than I recalled, a deeper, browner shade of red, more like a dark maroon. I didn't trust my memory, though, so I just let it go. Besides, it stood to reason that the contents were confirmed. For something this important, it would have to be routine.

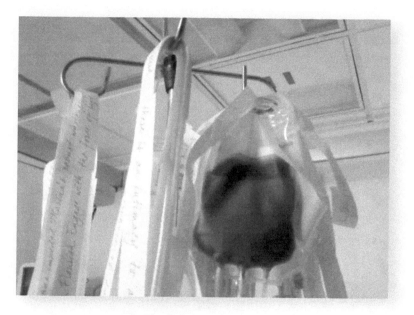

"Lars," Brigham and Women's Hospital, November 2012

15

Dimmers
of Hope

Marina's stem cell transplant didn't go the way we hoped. She was responding poorly—things had not gone well with Lars.

One week after New Year's Day, I was devoid of cheer. Marina's failing health was weighing heavy on my mind, and I was too distracted to be in a decent mood.

And yet, there was an optimistic tone to Sharon's posts. To me, this was confusing. Marina clearly wasn't well, and there weren't any signs that her condition would improve.

In any case, while Sharon's theme was "Don't give up the ship," all I heard was fiddling as seawater filled the hull. I couldn't shake the feeling that the iceberg had been hit.

APPROACHING BOSTON, I was in a melancholic daze. Marina was still struggling, and it wasn't looking good. My mind was full of questions. *Will there be a fix for this? What happened with the transplant? What if nothing can be done?*

I had become so lost in thought that I was missing turns. I think I even hit some unidentified debris.

"Pick a lane!" I shouted as I tried to pass a truck.

My anger was a thin disguise for fear I couldn't voice. I rarely lose my cool, but when I do, all hell breaks loose. And when I'm scared, it's even worse. I'm like a rabid dog.

Marina's newest symptom was a rash that ran amok. What made it problematic was that when it reared its head, it forced a change of plan involving doctors in New York. They were prepared to implement an all-new protocol, but were afraid to start until the rash could be contained.

Sharon shared the treatment plan. She made it sound routine.

"What set off the rash?" I asked. "Is this a common thing?"

"Transplants can cause rashes, but they're rarely this severe. She also wasn't taking her immune-suppressant drug."

"She wasn't? Why? I thought she *had* to take it. Didn't you?"

"Her New York doctor made the call on this. He's not concerned. They need her to abstain before her treatment can begin. Plus, they won't proceed until her rash has been addressed."

"Were you concerned that this would be a risky thing to do?"

"Her doctors didn't seem to be. It's only for three days. If all goes as we hope it will, she shouldn't skip a beat."

Marina's rash began to clear, but it came at a cost. Besides experiencing more discomfort and fatigue, she was requiring more assistance with her basic needs. Her doctor thought she needed time to rally from the rash, but sadly, after several days she only struggled more.

I met Sharon in the hall outside Marina's room.

"All right, fill me in," I said. "What happened? And what's next?"

"Her doctors are discussing it, but so far, they're perplexed."

"Perplexed? How reassuring! I don't get it. What's the deal?"

"They have a few more tests to run."

"So run the damn things, then!"

"These things take time."

"But why so long?"

"It's just the way it is. But since you're so impatient, what's your sense? Can you tune in?"

"I'm hesitant to go there, but I will, if you insist."

"Any thoughts you have right now are welcome. Be my guest."

"Okay," I sighed, "but don't forget, it's only food for thought."

"Thanks for the disclaimer," Sharon quipped.

"You bet," I said. "And now that I've decreased your expectations, here's the scoop. I think Marina had some kind of odd immune response. Which makes no sense because her donor cells were preapproved. In any case, that's my two cents, although, I must be wrong. Otherwise, this notion would have surely been explored."

"You're right," she said, "this makes no sense, but I'll see what they think. It never hurts to ask. You never know where it could lead."

Later, Sharon called to share the long-awaited news. As it turned out, Marina had graft-versus-host disease. From time to time, when donor cells, or grafts, are introduced, they fail to get along with cells residing in the host. Regrettably, an oversight appeared to play a role. The timeline and the details were a little hard to grasp, but in a nutshell, there were problems with Marina's care. It seemed that while the full-time staff was on their Christmas break, no one caught that her immune-suppressant was on hold. Apparently, the backup crew had not been made aware, and hence there was a lapse of time before it was resumed.

Although we couldn't quantify the damage that this caused,

it raised some thorny questions that were hard to brush aside. For instance, did the time lapse cause unalterable harm? Why was no one briefed about the timing for the drug? And what about Marina? Did she fail to notice too? Could she have missed the window for the drug to be resumed?

In the end, these questions would go largely unresolved. *You can't make sense of things that make no sense,* I told myself. But maybe—in some kind of quantum, otherworldly way—senseless things make sense in ways that no one can conceive?

Wishful thinking? Maybe so. Regardless, what's the harm? Besides, considering all the things we think make sense that don't, there must be ways in which it works the other way around. If not, I hope that God rethinks the way he set this up.

16

Sweet
Surrender

"Marina asked for you. Her mother said she's giving up."

To hear this was alarming. I could barely stay composed. My dad asked if I was okay. I couldn't even speak.

En route to Boston that same day, I was reduced to tears. I felt like I was drowning in a stormy sea of gloom. *It's not supposed to end this way,* I thought. *It isn't fair! There must be something else that can be done! She* can't *give up!*

But then I forced myself to sober up and face the truth. Sharon sounded very clear. Marina wanted out.

The night staff at the hospital had come to know my face. Although few words would be exchanged when I would come and go, I'd often feel encouraged by their waves and knowing nods. I told myself that each one meant, *I wish your loved one luck.* It gave me strength to think that they were conscious of my role, and that I wasn't just another stranger in the night.

I paused outside Marina's door. I had to catch myself. My instinct was to knock in an enthusiastic way, but given the occasion, I thought better and refrained.

A nurse looked up and smiled as I tapped lightly on the door. I listened for a moment, hoping I'd be welcomed in, but when no one responded, I began to get concerned. So sheepishly, I asked the gracious nurse to show me in—and said, "Just so you know, if they complain, this is on you."

I worried that the mood would be some manner of morose and that the weight of it would cast a pall on our exchange. Instead, I found Marina and her mom in an embrace. Face-to-face, in silence, they were sprawled atop her bed, appearing to be spellbound as they beamed each other love.

For several minutes, I discreetly watched them hold their gaze. Clearly, they were fluent in the language of the heart, which in this case did not require the use of any words.

I felt a bit uncomfortable and worried I'd intrude, so hoping that I wouldn't, I began to turn away. But when I did, Marina raised her head and looked my way. Then when Sharon noticed me, she told me to come in. I asked her if I should have stayed outside. She shook her head.

"We've been expecting you." She smiled.

"But I can wait," I said.

"No need," she said. "We're glad you're here. Come in. You're right on time."

"Okay," I said demurely. "You can always kick me out."

"I will," she teased. "Unless, somehow, you manage to behave."

"Behavior is subjective," I replied. "Marina knows. At any rate, what happens now? Where do we go from here?"

"Well," she said, "as you're aware, Marina's had enough. She's made it clear. She's letting go. It was a mindful choice."

"Part of me refuses to believe this," I replied. "I will, though, if I have to. Either way, what happens next?"

"Marina will get everything she needs to be at ease. But all she wants right now is love. That's why she asked for you."

"I'm here to give her that, and more," I sighed. "I'm glad she asked. The love is strong for this one. Like the Force, as Yoda said."

"She knows you'll be supportive, kind, and present," Sharon said, "and won't force her to question the decision that she's made. You also won't insist that she defend it. Others might. In view of this, she's only seeing people that she trusts."

Sharon left the room to let us have some time alone. It was appreciated. We had sentiments to share.

I took Marina's hand and placed it gently on my chest. Briefly, I was silent. I was too upset to speak.

"You've made your choice," I finally said. "The fight was never fair. You played your hand the best you could. Too bad the game was rigged."

"Who plays games that can't be won?" she said. "It's time to fold."

"It's hard to win with hands like yours. It was a lousy deal. It seems you've come to terms with this. I hope you feel relieved."

"I do. It's good to know that this will all be over soon. I've made my peace with letting go. I'm on to better things."

"I wish it could be different, though. I wish we could do more."

"The deck was stacked against me."

"Even though we bet the house?"

"You always have to trump me."

"And you always follow suit."

"That's because you deal me in."

"So now you'll cash your chips?"

"There's no bad time for cracking jokes, is there?" Marina said. "Thanks for that. No matter what, you always make me laugh."

"I won't quit my day job," I replied. "But back to you. Do you have any thoughts about what's going to happen next?"

"I'm going to the Cosmic Club of Everlasting Souls! And I'll send postcards, if I can, so look for them, okay?"

"Postcards, huh?" I chuckled. "How about a social call? But not when I'm *au naturel*. Or—"

"Thank you! Got the point."

"Anyway, I think you're right. There must be something more. But even so, I'll keep the shreds of hope that I have left. Besides, I know you've booked your trip, but flights can be delayed. Or *canceled*. It could happen! Flights get canceled all the time! Perhaps you'll heal spontaneously? Why not? You never know!"

"A miracle is fine," Marina said, "if it's my fate. But if it's not, so be it. I've made peace with letting go."

"But miracles are fluky and unlikely," I replied. "In my view, something less extreme—and rare—could still occur. It might be wishful thinking, but I *can't* just count you out!"

There was a short—and painful—pause. She smiled. I swallowed hard.

"I'm sorry," I continued. "This is all still sinking in."

My eyes welled up with tears as she reached out to grasp my hand. And then, in silence, I began to gently stroke her hair. She'd trained me well. I knew the drill. Head first, then hands, then feet.

"You know . . . someday, we'll *all* be dead," I said. "We live, we die. And it's not length but depth and breadth that will define a life. And you nailed that part, didn't you? You lived your life out loud. While others hemmed and hawed, you oohed and aahed. *You* lived it up."

"I guess you're right," Marina said. "I always faced my fears. My friends thought I was brave to try so many daring things, but I was really just afraid of dying with regrets. I'm sure you can relate to this. I know you've taken risks. I hope that you'll do more brave things, and trust that it's okay."

"Brave or stupid?" I replied. "For me, the line is fine."

Marina smiled, and helped herself to something for her pain. Clearly, it was working. She was lucid and serene.

"Are you afraid to die?" she asked.

"Are *you*?"

"I asked you first."

"To me, death is a comma. Periods are a mirage."

"What about the afterlife?"

"An exclamation point!"

"You think?" she sighed.

"I do." I laughed. "Despite my doubtful brain. Because there is a part of me that's absolutely sure. The same part that receives—and trusts—the insights that I share."

"Do you know what the Other Side is like?" Marina asked. "And is there just *one* Other Side? Could there be Other *Sides*? Where, exactly, do we go? And what can we expect?"

"We booked you on a first-class flight to paradise," I said.

"More legroom, right?" she quipped. "I hope it's not a bumpy flight."

"It won't be. Astral planes have stabilizers. Liquor too."

"Do astral planes fly just to astral planes?"

"And JFK."

"I like that airport!" she exclaimed. "They have spa treatments there. But you ignored my question. Honestly, where do we go?"

"It's hard to ponder things we can't imagine," I replied. "Most of all, when it involves the end of all we've known. We also view the Other Side from *this* side, which is blurred. I mean while we're still in the flesh, consumed with scary thoughts. For instance, that we could end up in some eternal void. But if we *do* survive our death, why would this be the case? And why would we perceive things there the same as we do here? And if we don't, then what becomes of judgment, pain, and fear? My guess is that these kinds of things aren't issues anymore."

"I hope you're right," she said. "I'll let you know when I find out. But I'd still like to have a sense of what it might be like."

I grabbed Marina's laptop to find Afterlife TV. My friend—and former private eye—Bob Olson is the host. He also was a skeptic whose dad passed when he was young. His focus on the afterlife was prompted by this loss. He uses his fact-finding skills to weigh compelling claims and to confirm reports that life continues when we die.

"Here it is," I said. "Bob Olson's Afterlife TV."

"Hi there, Bob," Marina said. "I've only heard good things."

"Bob helps people lose their fear that life ends when we die. He wants to give us hope—and even proof—that life goes on. He shares accounts of stories that appear to be legit. It might be good to hear a few. I think you'll be impressed."

We watched assorted interviews and stopped to share our thoughts. The questions posed by Bob were like the ones we asked ourselves.

"Why do children sometimes mention prior lives?" I asked. "People, scenes, and languages they've never even heard! And then there are the mediums. The honest ones, I mean. Some are too specific and consistent to dismiss."

"You're right." She nodded. "Like *you* are. But you read people cold. And don't ask any questions. It's uncommon, I assume."

"I also like to give specific details," I replied. "For instance, grandson, overdose, was twenty when he passed. A star tattoo, blue eyes, brown hair, and scars on his right leg. I'll get a name sometimes as well, which can be in *reverse*. E-g-r-o-e-g, George. Don't ask me why, or how."

"Hmm," she said. "Why backward? Oops. You said I

couldn't ask. Anyway, thank Bob for me. I feel more hopeful now."

"I'm glad you had a chance to hear the interviews," I said. "Some of them were out there—in a good way—don't you think? The one with Dr. Brian Weiss impressed me most of all. When he regressed his patient, what she said took him aback. She gave him information that she had no knowledge of, including that his infant son lived only for a month. And that his heart was *backward* and his arteries reversed! She also knew his Hebrew name was Avrom. Crazy, right? The woman didn't know a thing about Judaic names, nor had she been briefed about his background or his life.

"There's also the Moorjani case. Extraordinary, huh? Anita's doctors had lost hope. Her cancer was advanced. And then, while on her deathbed, she perceived a higher place. She also saw some relatives who'd been deceased for years, who told her that it wasn't time for her to join them yet. And then, against all odds, she was restored to perfect health! There was no intervention! Shortly after, she was healed. Skeptics roll their eyes when they catch wind of tales like this. But how can *every* one be a coincidence or hoax? Carl Jung said something once that speaks to this. To paraphrase: it's foolish to discredit everything we can't explain."

Marina yawned and looked like she could use a little sleep. Only then was I aware that it was 2 a.m.

"It's late," Marina said. "Go home. Don't worry. I'll be fine. Besides, once I cross over, I'll be sure to let you know. In fact, if you would like a sign, I'll see what I can do."

"A sign?" I laughed. "Well, since you asked, I'd like a billboard please."

"I mean it, though! I'll send a sign. I really will! You'll see!"

"I'd love a sign, as long as it's not something indistinct. Your face on toast, for instance, or a cloud shaped like your head."

"That wouldn't do it for you, huh?" She smiled. "Choose something then."

"Hold on!" I snapped. "I need to *think . . .*"

"*Balloon ball! That's* your sign."

"My sign is a *baboon call*? I don't think so. Try again. Do you know what they sound like? I don't even have a clue."

"I said *balloon* ball, Einstein!" she exclaimed. "You're such a dork!"

At least, I thought, *it's novel. But she has her work cut out. There's no such thing! Like leprechauns. And fairies. And free lunch.*

17

The Last
Farewell

*I*t was March 10. A sunless Sunday. It was apropos.

"I'm still in shock," my mother said. "This wasn't in the script. I didn't see it coming. How can life be so unfair?"

"Fate is fickle," I replied, "and isn't always fair. The lesson is that no one is immune to tragic things."

En route to see Marina, I was in a sober mood. With me were my parents, Cheryl, and my brother Paul, and as we turned our thoughts to her, it was with heavy hearts.

As family outings go, I thought, *there's no upside to this.*

"At my wedding," Paul remarked, "she seemed so full of life."

"I know," I said. "She was at ours as well, as I recall."

"But *mine* was not that long ago. It's been a while since yours!"

"Oh. You mean it's strange to think it hasn't been that long?"

"Should I be talking slower? Do I need to dumb it down?"

"Don't provoke him." Cheryl laughed. "He's sensitive, you know. Not that you should be concerned. He wouldn't hurt a flea."

"Wouldn't hurt a flea?" Paul said. "He's really got you fooled!"

"You only got what you deserved." I groused. "In hindsight, less."

As we approached the hospital, the conversation ebbed. Until then, our exchanges, while amusing, were short-lived, and mainly station breaks for what was playing in our heads. But once our destination was in view, all bets were off. Reality was setting in to wake us from the fog.

Sharon met us in the lobby after we arrived. "Marina is

asleep," she said, "and should be waking soon. But when you see her, be prepared. She's in a fragile state."

I could tell my dad was tense. He was on foreign ground. If something yanks his heartstrings, he retreats to friendly soil. This time, though, I wasn't sure that he could pull it off. He'd have to shut his eyes and block his ears. And close his heart.

Marina smiled when we arrived. We gathered near her bed. To see her look so frail and withered shook me to the core. It worried me to think that she might see it on my face.

I hugged her very gently, trying not to look upset.

"Are you okay?" I asked, as if my question wasn't lame.

She grabbed my hand and held it. "Don't go anywhere," she said. Then she greeted Cheryl, Paul, my mother, and my dad.

He seems inhibited, I thought. *I hope he loosens up.*

My dad appeared unsettled as he stooped to give his hug, but when Marina noticed, she decided to respond. After whispering something just the two of them could hear, she snatched his reading glasses from the pocket of his shirt. Then she put them on, sat up in bed, and raised her voice.

"Hello, my name is Curt!" she joked. "I have four kooky sons. I love my boat and good cigars. My wife is awesome too!"

Right away, my dad appeared to be more comfortable. And then I thought, *It's plain to see what prompted her response.* Marina noticed that my dad was feeling out of sorts. But rather than pretend she couldn't tell, she made a joke. She knew that he'd feel reassured if she could make him laugh and that her loving gesture would put everyone at ease.

After we told stories, shared our thoughts, and reminisced, I asked to see Marina with just Cheryl in the room. As Sharon cleared the space, a lump was forming in my throat. I swallowed hard, and thought, *It's time. We have to say good-bye.*

"Well, kid," I said. "I hope that you're prepared to turn the page. The upside is that you'll be spared from hearing all my jokes."

As Cheryl held Marina's hand, I softly stroked her hair.

"All of us will die," I said. "There's no escaping this. But leaving on an early flight might not be all that bad. Maybe all it means is that your work is finished here? Perhaps you learned so much, so fast, that you're just skipping grades? Old souls are the brightest. They learn quickly and move on. But *new* souls—folks like me—are slow. We have to stay behind."

"But Cheryl is an old soul too," she sighed, "and *she's* still here."

"Sure." I laughed. "But no one knows how soon she'll have to leave!"

"When would soon be?" she replied. "Tomorrow? Fifty years? How are you defining soon? Who told you how this works?"

"See?" I said. "I'm not that wise. That's why I have to stay. I might be in the second grade. You have a PhD."

Marina smiled as Cheryl shook her head. "*First* grade," she said.

"Anyway," I sighed, "I hope the rainbow measures up. Remember all the things we talked about? Amazing, right?"

I thought about our many chats regarding life and death, and how the stories we discussed provided strength and hope. I hoped that she remembered and was comforted by them.

Marina's eyes began to close. It seemed she needed rest. We waited. Minutes later, she appeared to be confused.

"I feel strange," she sighed.

"How so?" I said.

"I can't explain."

"Are you okay?"

"I'm just . . . surprised. And at a loss for words."

I wondered if her weary brain was starting to play tricks. Some believe that when a person is this close to death, a neural process can take place that prompts delusive thoughts. But a near-death experience is harder to explain. Also known as NDEs, they are unique events. Those who have them feel they go to some transcendent place and have the kinds of insights that delusions can't provide. Plus, they often see themselves from higher points of view, and hear discussions—in detail—that happen far away.

Accounts of this phenomenon have been described like this: A woman who is close to death describes her NDE. She claims that she had access to an otherworldly place, and noticed that a shoe was on a ledge above her room. Then, when someone goes to look, they find that she was right. The shoe could not be seen from windows, buildings, or the ground, and yet she knew how it appeared, and what floor it was on.

Things like this are too compelling to be written off. How do people see things that are distant or obscured, especially when they're close to death or in an altered state?

"Boss," I sighed, "we have to say good-bye. At least for now. But if you need me, let me know. Just tell your mom to call."

Marina closed her eyes again and seemed to drift away. Then, for several minutes, she appeared to glow with bliss.

"Are you with us, kid?" I asked. "If not, stay where you are. I hope that peaceful look I see reflects the way you feel."

"It does," Marina softly said. "I really can't explain. But I feel bathed in warmth and love, and have a sense of peace."

"A glimpse of what's to come?" I said. "I say we go with that."

"Yes," she said. "We'll go with that. I wish I could say more."

"We'll reconvene in paradise," I said, "when I arrive. And when I do, I hope you'll organize the meet and greet."

"Yes, I will. I promise. I'll be there to guide you in."

"Good. You'll be the sentinel at heaven's pearly gate."

A nurse heard this and left in tears. I heard Marina sigh.

"And if you see Saint Pete," I said.

"I'll plead your case," she vowed.

Her voice trailed off. I noticed Cheryl wipe away some tears.

And then my mind became consumed with agitated thoughts. *What a twisted, pointless script! This can't be how it goes! Where's the silver lining? What about the pot of gold? What's the point of being here if this is how it ends?*

"Marina, get some rest," I sighed.

"I love you," she replied.

"I love you *more*. We'll see you . . . well . . . we'll see you when we do."

"I know you will. I love you both."

"And don't forget my sign."

"Balloon ball," she said softly.

"Yup, good luck with that," I said.

I took her hand and kissed her on the forehead several times.

"Save a few for Cheryl," she replied.

"Will do." I smiled.

As she began to drift away, we lingered by her side. We had to leave, but couldn't bear to go. It was too hard.

And then, as I released her hand, our eyes met one last time.

"We love you," Cheryl whispered.

"*More*," I said. "We always will."

Marina smiled serenely as she floated back to sleep. And as she did, we turned away, and forced ourselves to leave.

I hurried to a restroom, trying hard to stay composed. And then, while rushing to a stall, the tears began to flow. While wiping them away, I thought, *Fuck fate! Fuck cancer too!*

I heard a laugh outside the stall.

Fuck you, I almost said.

18

Graduation
Day

The twelfth of March—a Tuesday—proved to be a fateful day. Marina's hourglass would spill its final grains of sand.

Your mind can play strange tricks when you await a loved one's death. For instance, you might feel removed, or even strangely numb. This was my experience the day Marina passed. Perhaps it was because it seemed too painful to be true.

The day before, some friends arrived to see her one last time. One was moved to sing and play some songs on her guitar and had her spirit lifted when Marina sang along.

I wondered if she knew that she would never sing again. If so, I can't imagine how it felt to take this in. For instance, I can't fathom having one last favorite meal, or doing anything I treasured for a final time. I'm not sure I'd enjoy it much. This wasn't true for her.

Marina also asked her mom if she could go outside, so Sharon found a wheelchair, and they went for one last stroll. With rays of sunlight streaming down to warm her weary face, she savored every precious, fleeting moment she had left. This was how she lived her life. With presence and intent. She didn't waste a minute. Every moment was a gift.

Some photos Sharon sent me captured moods throughout the day. There were no hints of doom and gloom or any signs of fear. The room had been transformed, it seemed, into a sacred space.

I also spied a photo of Marina's purple nails. Her cousin April painted them for her the day before.

Of course, I thought, *Marina chose to leave this world in style. I'm not surprised. She wouldn't do it any other way.*

I did consider visiting Marina once again, but in the end, decided it would be a selfish choice. Time was precious now, and I'd already said good-bye. As painful as it was, I knew my chance had come and gone.

As Marina's life force waned, her loved ones held her close. While gathered near her bed, they gently stroked her hands and feet, and shared a range of sentiments that warmed Marina's heart. They also laughed, told jokes, sang songs, and even did some chants. With mindful thoughts and tender words, they filled the room with love.

Later, unexpectedly, a special friend arrived. Phil Wald had helped his brother, Michael, with Marina's care. Michael was an integrated health practitioner whose focus was attending to nutritional concerns. His guidance was invaluable at many crucial points, and Phil's relaxed demeanor often eased Marina's fears. When told about her status, Phil was moved to say good-bye and took the long drive from New York to see her one last time.

Marina's favorite nurse took special pains to be there too. Nancy rearranged her shifts that week with her in mind.

As day turned into night, Marina whispered her last words.

"Are we ready, Mom?" she slurred.

"When you are," Sharon sighed.

"Good. Are my nails ready?"

"They sure are!"

"Then I am too."

Sharon smiled and watched Marina close her weary eyes. As she appeared to fade into a deep state of repose, her loved ones held her gently, bathing her with loving thoughts. Then it wasn't long before she took her final breath. At half past seven, at long last, Marina Day was free.

PART

11

The Times
of the Signs

19

At One in the Mourning

"I want to help my generation find deeper, more connected relationships and meaning for their lives. I want to travel. I want to see everything, learn everything. I want to make eye contact with people who walk past me on the street. I want to say 'Hello, how are you?' and truly care about what they say."

—MARINA DAY

When those we love depart this life, we can't know how we'll feel. We know that we'll be sad, but depths of grief can't be foreseen. And grief sneaks up on us. It comes and goes in stealthy waves. The moment we assume we're safe, a swell can take us down.

Meanwhile, in the wake of loss, the waves kept rolling in. It made me seek distractions. They were respites. Sadness breaks.

All the contact that I had with Sharon was by text. I didn't call because I was afraid she needed space. Texting let me stay in touch, but on respectful terms. It also let me screen my thoughts before they left my head.

Email also did the trick when I felt moved to vent. Here's one I wrote to Sharon when the waves were at their peak:

Sharon . . . I hope you're okay. I thought I should check in.

Yesterday, I had a run of sad and angry thoughts. The insights it provided were invaluable to me. In case you're interested, here's an excerpt from my notes:

Why do people think that tragedies are acts of God? And that there is a purpose for the things that cause us pain? And that we only get what we can handle. Or deserve!

I've had enough of these clichés. Since when do they prove true? When someone dies from cancer, have they handled what they faced? And what's the point of handling things if God just hands us more? What's the motivation? Who would even want to try?

Clearly, I've had feelings that I've needed to express.

Along with lots of questions. Like, what is our purpose here?

Perhaps we're here to learn to love and come to terms with loss? I just wish that our lessons didn't come at such a cost.

But as the fog lifts—by degrees—between the waves of grief, my sorrow pales compared to what I can take comfort in. Because—despite how hard it is to bear Marina's loss—the gift of having known her is an ever-lasting one. To know her was to love her, and that love will never die.

For now, though, sharing how we feel is what will help us heal. The grief we share is grief we spare. We can't heal pain alone.

THE WAVES OF grief were fierce on March 19 at 1 a.m. Relentlessly, they billowed as I lay awake in bed, and I began to wonder if they ever would subside. I tried, repeatedly, to change the channel in my head, but every station seemed to play the same tear-jerking flick.

I grabbed a book, but couldn't keep my mind on what I read. So I reached for the laptop on the table near my bed—and when I raised the lid of it, here's what was on the screen.

Marina's photo. Nothing else, except an inquiry. It was below the photo. Just three words: *Are you awake?*

I wondered how this could appear, from nowhere, on my screen. The date marked on the photo was one month before she died. So why was it appearing now? And when did it get sent?

I didn't hit a switch or key, and all my apps were closed. I couldn't fathom any way that this could have occurred.

So then I went to Facebook. Something told me I should check. I wondered if Marina sent a message that I missed. But then I thought, *In any case, why is it on my screen?*

As it turned out, her note was there, but it was marked unread. And strangely, there appeared to be no photograph attached.

I'd visited my Facebook page at frequent intervals, so it was odd that I had never seen it there before. And odd that it was the *one thing* I missed each time I looked.

When Cheryl stirred, she saw me staring blankly at the screen.

"What are you looking at?" she asked.

"Um . . . something strange," I said.

"Aren't you *always*—"

"Not *this* strange . . ."

"What is it?"

"Take a look."

I pointed to the photo of Marina on my screen, and paused before attempting to explain how it appeared.

"Her photo—and her *message*—came from nowhere!" I exclaimed. "I didn't even think that I had left my laptop on! So how did it get on my screen? It's crazy, don't you think?"

"Crazy?" Cheryl bellowed. "Is *that* what you think it is? Marina promised you a sign! Hello? She's checking in!"

She rolled her eyes, turned on her side, and promptly fell asleep. I wondered how. A lesser thing could keep me up for days.

I thought to save a screenshot to confirm that I was sane. And then I did a shout out to Marina in my head.

Kiddo, if this came from you, I thought, *I need a sign! So where's the one you promised me? I thought we had a deal!*

20

The Purple Hat

Another week had passed without a postcard from my niece. I did see *pictures* of balloons. A few were purple too. But I refused to take the bait. It had to be a fluke.

Purple was Marina's favorite color, by the way, so I assumed that this was why they even caught my eye. Besides, I bargained for a more persuasive form of proof. For instance, what I learned from Sharon later in the week. She told me that Marina's friend Marissa was in touch, and had exciting news that she was eager to reveal.

"She kept her word!" Marissa said. "Marina sent a sign!"

As it turned out, Marissa asked Marina for one too.

But this was not the only thing that I was shocked to hear. I also learned that signs were promised to Marina's friends. Specifically, Marissa and Daniela. That was it.

As much as it surprised me to receive this piece of news, what I discovered later bordered on beyond belief.

Twin brothers, Trey and Nick, were in Marina's circle too. They had been told about the sign Marina planned to send, and made a point to bring their mother, Susan, up to speed.

As luck would have it, this disclosure proved fortuitous. Shortly after, Susan chanced upon Marissa's sign. She noticed it while caring for the daughter of a friend. Together with some items that were in her daughter's room, Susan was surprised to find a weathered purple hat. "Marina came to mind," she said, "because she fancied hats, but what made this one special was the way it was inscribed!"

Later, Susan asked her friend about the purple hat. Strangely, she did not recall the origin of it. Nor was she aware that it was in her daughter's room.

When Susan asked to borrow it, her friend gave her consent.

Trey and Nick will be surprised to see this. Susan mused. *And when Marissa sees it, she'll be even more surprised!*

Susan placed the hat beside an angel figurine and snapped a photo of it that she texted to her sons. And then she promptly sent the photo to Marissa, too, along with a communiqué about where it was found.

Predictably, the photo took Marissa's breath away. "Leave it to Marina!" she exclaimed. "She kept her word! She loved the color purple and was fond of wearing hats! But what I'm most impressed by is what's printed on the front! Could anything be any more convincing? Or distinct?"

It's hard to fathom how this could have been a happenstance, especially considering what was printed on the hat. Marina's *name* was on the front. Her first name *and* her last.

The purple hat, Marissa's sign

So let's review the details, just to drive the story home. Her signature apparel? Check. Her favorite color? Check. First and last name on the hat? Another check. A fluke?

Perhaps, but here's the clincher, just in case you're not convinced. Marina asked Marissa what she wanted for a sign, but after thinking long and hard, one didn't come to mind. Marina said, "Don't worry. I'll send something really clear. You'll know without a doubt that it's from me and meant for you."

As it turned out, the sign came at the perfect time and place. Marissa noticed Susan's text while chatting with a friend. The topic was Marina. And what kind of sign she'd send.

21

Balloonacy

Another week had passed, and time still hadn't healed a thing. Marina had been in my mind, and heart, around the clock.

The waves of grief were more persistent than I had foreseen, and my attempts to ride them were like surfing in a rip. I did my best, but every time I'd get swept out to sea. It made me wonder if I'd ever see the shore again.

Of course, it would have helped to be in contact with my niece. Any kind of interaction would have done the trick, as long as it was clear enough for me to see or hear. But then I thought, *To hear her voice would be the best surprise.* I missed it, and I wondered why she hadn't been in touch.

In lieu of this, I chose to play some songs from her CD. I then recalled that one described the joy of chap-free lips, and laughed when I discovered that she called it "Stick De Chap."

But hearing it, I thought, *might make me miss her even more.*

So after contemplating it, I put the disc aside. But then, of course, I had another not-so-bright idea. It was to watch Marina sing by viewing YouTube clips. Sure enough, I found a list of songs that she'd performed, and chose a few to listen to. At least that's what I thought.

Apparently, I clicked on something other than her clips. What played instead appeared to have no relevance to her.

I saw a group of people gathered in an open field. I also noticed they were holding helium balloons. At first, it wasn't clear to me what their intention was. And then I learned that they were paying tribute to a friend. Releasing the balloons was how they chose to let him go.

What made me click on this? I thought. *And why would it be here? I thought I chose a song Marina wrote. It makes no sense.*

I thought about this later as I tossed and turned in bed.

I'm clearly overthinking this. I need to get some sleep.

And then the sheep that I was counting morphed into balloons.

"GOOD MORNING, HONEY!" Cheryl chirped. "Did I just wake you up?"

"Nope," I groaned. "I'm comatose and talking in my sleep."

"Stop your nonsense!" she exclaimed. "You need to look outside!"

I argued, kicked the covers off, and staggered out of bed.

"You're like a mule!" she bellowed.

"No, I'm not."

"You're kidding, right?"

"Compared to you, I'm docile and compliant. Even meek."

As I trudged to the window, Cheryl pointed to a tree. Hanging on a branch was an attention-grabbing orb. As it turned out, it was a round, carnation-pink balloon.

"Well?" she said. "Try doubting this! Marina sent your sign!"

"It's just a pink balloon," I groused. "I'm going back to bed."

"But wait! When have you seen balloons—in trees—in our backyard? Or messages—with photos—from departed relatives?"

"All right, relax! *Balloon ball* was our sign. Not pink balloon!"

"It has to be a sign! C'mon! How likely would it be? Could it be accidental that it's in your line of sight?"

"My wife is a balloonatic!" I snapped. "I won't be, though. I know you think I'm stubborn, but I'm just not that impressed."

"Why not?" she said. "What's wrong with you? You trust your instincts, right? How could you have any doubts that it's Marina's sign?"

"Marina told me that she'd send a special sign," I said. "That was our deal. Remember? We discussed it several times. Besides, Marissa got a hat! A goddamn *purple* one! It even had Marina's name stitched on the goddamn front! And it was found well over thirty miles from where she lived! So since she's so damn good at this, she can do better, right?"

"Argggh! How stubborn can you be? Marina sent your sign! She shouldn't have to work so hard. C'mon! Give her a break!"

"A break? She's in the promised land! Why would she need a break?"

"Then how will she convince you? Will she have to *resurrect*?"

"I want my sign. The one she said she'd send. But first things first. Let's see if there's a ball below, or somewhere near the tree. If so, we can revisit this. If not, this case is closed."

Again, I was immovable, as mules are known to be. I also was a little miffed about the purple hat. *If she can pull that off,* I thought, *why would she make* me *wait?* And yet, there was Marina's note and photo on my screen. It was no wonder Cheryl thought that I was hard to please.

And no, there were no balls of any kind around the tree. Cheryl did a thorough search. "Round stones don't count," I quipped.

22

The Memorial
at Pine Lake

The plan was for two celebrations of Marina's life. The first one would be held at Bard—on campus—in New York, and the ensuing one would be in Georgia at Pine Lake.

Pine Lake had been Marina's home since she was six years old. Close to 700 people occupy this town, where residents enjoy a quiet, unpretentious life. It's also a communal place that favors living green, and though it's near Atlanta, when you're there, it feels remote.

In an eco-friendly home a stone's throw from the lake, Marina figured that she lived in paradise on earth. The tiny lake is charming in a folksy sort of way and serves as an idyllic spot to spend a summer day. In fact, it was Marina's favorite place to meet her friends, and where they gathered frequently for cozy fireside chats. It also was where she would dream about a gentler world and vow to share her vision of the change she hoped to see.

Marina's tribute would be on the fourth and fifth of May, but since I had commitments on the fifth, I couldn't stay. It meant I'd be arriving on the morning of the fourth and leaving on an evening flight to Boston that same day.

On the morning of the trip, I woke at 5 a.m. To my dismay, I had a very short and restless sleep. I spent the whole night pondering the purpose of my trip. The good news, though, was that I didn't have to go alone. Cheryl kindly volunteered to be my chaperone.

Once we were on board the plane, I slumped into my seat. I hoped that I'd be able to relax—and even sleep—but in my restless state of mind, it proved too hard to do. At least the time went quickly. It was just a two-hour flight. And then, before we knew it, we were off to find Pine Lake.

As we approached the lake where the memorial would be, I wondered if Marina would be there in some way too. If so, I also wondered what her vantage point would be. Would she be "looking down on us" as people like to think? Or there, but not in any way or form we could conceive? I hoped that if she did attend, she'd offer us a hint.

"If I know her," I joked, "we'll see a rainbow. Or a dove. And then the dove will splatter us with tidings of good cheer."

Sharon beamed when we arrived, and gave a welcome wave. She looked relieved to see us. It was good to see her smile. It made me think of all the times that I came to her aid, most often at the hospital when something went awry. The standing joke was that I was the second wave of troops, and was called in to storm the beach and steel Marina's will. I sighed and wished a discharge could have been arranged instead. And then a wave of grief rolled in too quickly to conceal. I tried to disregard it, but it was to no avail. As tears were welling in my eyes, I had to turn away.

After seeing Sharon, I talked privately with Mike. He seemed to be a little dazed, or hesitant to speak, although I wasn't certain how objective I could be. Perhaps, since I was in a daze, I figured he was too. I often thought about him when Marina wasn't well, and wondered if he felt cut off or powerless to help. Any time I saw him, I would make a point to ask, but often sensed he might be disconnected from his truth, as if his psyche chose to keep some feelings in reserve. If this *was* the case, I thought it might be how he coped. I might have even done the same if I'd been in his shoes.

Once we saw more relatives and met Marina's friends, Cheryl left with Sharon for a walk around the lake. After talking to my aunt, I hustled to catch up, regretting that I had to miss a part of Sharon's tour. Then, while pointing out the spots Marina loved the most, she told us several stories that we'd never heard before. Some were funny, others fun to hear. A few were sad. I found them sad because they made me miss her even more.

Later, Sharon gathered everyone to wrap things up. "If anyone has thoughts to share," she said, "this is the time." But it was late, and I realized we had to catch a plane.

"Will this take long?" I asked someone. "What's going to happen next? If we don't leave, we'll miss our plane! I know, bad timing, right? I'd love to hear the stories, though, and maybe tell some too. Nonetheless, I bet Marina had a say in this. She probably insisted that we all have time to speak!"

I then heard Sharon saying, "Now it's Michael's turn to speak."

This took me by surprise. I thought she might have changed her mind. I'd asked to speak when we arrived, but she told me to wait. She wanted those arriving late to hear what I would say.

"Speak!" she said.

"About Marina, right?" I shyly joked.

Some family members chuckled as I stood and wiped my brow. I then asked Sharon if the cameras could be put away. To me, they were distracting. One more thing to cloud my mind.

I didn't think I'd have to work so hard to stay composed. I hoped to say some funny, wise, or thought-provoking things, but all that came to mind was how surreal the moment seemed. And then I felt inspired to talk about Marina's signs. The note and photo that appeared on my computer screen. The pink balloon that Cheryl noticed hanging from a tree. The purple hat that had Marina's name stitched on the front. And then the sign Marina chose that I had yet to see.

"Marina has sent signs," I said. "So don't forget to look. Be patient, though. These things take time. I can attest to this."

23

Signing In

*The brightest rainbows are a
product of the darkest storms.*

THURSDAY, MAY 9, 2013
6:42 A.M.

I yawned as golden rays of sun beamed warmly on my face. Our bedroom was aglow with effervescent morning light, and as it streamed into the room, I heaved a comfy sigh.

And then I wondered why I hadn't thought to close the blinds. It was too early to wake up. At least it was for me.

I sat upright to see outside. The sky was bright and clear. Shafts of sunlight danced upon the surface of the lake, and as I watched it glisten, I was lulled by the effect.

Cheryl stirred, and seemed surprised to see that I was up.

"Good morning!" she said brightly as she bounded out of bed.

"I think there's something wrong with you," I groaned.

"With *me*?" she said.

"Yes! With *you*. You wake so fast!"

"And why is that so bad?"

"Because you pop right up. Like toast!"

"Like *normal* people do."

"What makes you think that's normal?"

"Well, it is compared to *you*!"

I'm a night owl through and through. It's how I've always been. But Cheryl is a lark who favors rising with the birds, so this means when she's up, I'm down, and when she's out, I'm in. Except, of course, for when I can't—or she won't let me—sleep.

As she tiptoed away, I thought, *It's strange we get along.* But then, I mused, *She's caring, bright, and easy on the eyes.* And as for me, I drew a blank. *I'll sleep on this,* I thought.

☆

AS CHERYL SCOOTED up the stairs, the noise jarred me awake. As she rushed in, I glared at her.

"You woke me up!" I barked.

"I have to talk to you!" she said.

"This instant? Can't it wait?"

"It can't! It's too important!"

"How important? Seriously. Unless . . . is it the rapture? Were you robbed? Did someone die?"

"No! Shut up! I have to tell you something! Can I? *Please!*"

I rolled my eyes and shook my head, as Cheryl set the scene:

"I left the house at 9 a.m. to walk around the lake and had to shield my eyes because the sunlight was so bright. In fact, it was so vivid that it made the surface gleam. And then, when I stopped walking—to appreciate the view—I noticed there was something skimming briskly toward the shore. At first I thought it was a swan, but quickly ruled it out. I doubted that a swan would be reflecting so much light."

"Go on," I said. "I'm listening. Does this story have an end?"

"All right be patient!" Cheryl snapped. "I'm getting there, okay? Anyway, it headed toward the clearing at the bend. As I moved closer to it, it stopped moving for a while, but then a gust of wind kicked up and pushed it toward the shore. And then the strangest thing occurred. I swear this is the truth! Once it reached the shoreline, it began to slowly rise, and as it did, the wind propelled it right into my hands. I didn't even have to reach, or move from where I stood!"

Then at last, she showed me what she had behind her back. I sat up slowly, certain that my eyes were playing tricks. Once I was convinced they weren't, I had to catch my breath.

Cheryl giggled as she watched me struggle to respond.

"Well?" she squealed. "It's your balloon ball, right? It *has* to be! It looks just like a beach ball with a smaller ball inside! It's also *round*. Balloons are almost always teardrop shaped! At first I thought it had to be a crazy stroke of luck, but then, once I composed myself, I thought about the odds. How could something so unique be a *coincidence*? And then I said out loud, 'Marina, thank you! Sign received!'"

I gaped in disbelief at the unorthodox balloon. And then my thoughts began to blur. *Is this for real?* I mused. *Is this what Cheryl thinks it is? Or what it seems to be?*

But then I thought, *This is absurd. I'm grasping straws again. Besides, the point is moot. Fictitious things can't be confirmed!*

Then I noticed something in small print on the balloon. A reference to the company that manufactured it. Without delay, I grabbed my phone to do a Google search, and found a vendor's home page, where this statement caught my eye:

We are a supplier of the world's best round balloons.
Resembling balls or bubbles, people call them **ball balloons**.

I give! I thought. *Soul-bump me, kid! You did it! Promise kept!*

The other signs were curious, but this one sealed the deal. Why, and how, had all of them appeared the way they did? Photos didn't just show up on my computer screen. I hadn't seen Marina's name on any purple hats, and no balloons were ever found in trees around our home. I also doubt balloons were being spotted in the lake. Surely none that floated to a person on the shore, and looked more like a beach ball than a typical balloon.

It makes me wonder how a skeptic would account for this. I mean the kind whose mind is, for the most part, welded shut. I bet he'd say that we're inclined to notice what we seek. Confirmation bias. Wishful thinking that proves true. In other words, we look for things to prove our false beliefs. Common things that otherwise would fail to catch our eye. Balloon balls, for example, which, of course, are drawn to lakes. Or purple hats with someone's first and last name on the front. Or messages on laptop screens from loved ones whom we've lost.

Besides, if expectations draw us to the things we seek, why do people fail when they expect to find success? Or Bigfoot, Waldo, peace of mind, nirvana, or a job? Or better yet, an everlasting cure for a disease? In general, though, I'm happy just to find my missing keys. And extra happy when I find a message from my niece.

24

Afterthoughts

Centered on the mantel in our bedroom is an urn. The urn contains some of the ashy remnants of my niece.

They were dispersed among her family members and some friends. Some had planned to scatter them in places that she loved. Others planned to put them in a locket or a charm, or sail to an exotic place and cast them to the sea.

Keepsakes that remind us of a loss can make us sad, but they can reacquaint us with auspicious memories too. Memories that inspire us to find joy in simple things, in part by helping us recall the way our loved ones lived.

And yet, sometimes these memories fade, and even disappear. For me, it tends to be when I hear disconcerting news. It causes me to question things it's hard to reconcile, like what makes people do bad things, and what's our purpose here? And when I do, Marina's death takes on a darker hue. Her loss feels even harder to accept and comprehend.

The upside is that these digressions tend to be short-lived. And when they're not, a mantra puts me back on solid ground. In fact, the one that I'm partial to goes more or less like this: *Balloon ball . . . purple hat . . . balloon in tree . . . are you awake?* Or now and then, in lieu of this: *We're more than we may seem.*

Marina's mantra. She was right. She proved it to me too.

I FASTENED THE balloon ball to the cover of the urn. Now and then, as I stroll by, I'll tap it with my hand, as if I were high-fiving her across the great divide. I'll also tap the urn sometimes and even lift the lid. Perhaps the kid in me still thinks that wishes can come true, and hopes Marina's spirit

—like a genie—might pop out. Or wants to think that he can rub the urn and wish her back.

At times, I do it to recall how fragile life can be. The urn piques my awareness that our days are numbered here, and that we never know how long we have until they're up.

Thankfully, my fears are eased when I see the balloon. It serves as a reminder that, as short as life may seem, it may just be a chapter in a book that never ends.

Let's say it's true. Imagine that we have immortal souls and live again, repeatedly, in many different forms. And that our lifetimes are like chapters, all with different themes. Today, as I consider this and think about *my* life, I realize that my greatest challenge was my greatest gift. It was—forgive the platitude—a blessing in disguise.

It also made me mindful of an escalating trend. As we've become distracted by the details of our lives, it's weakened our connection to the things that matter most. Relationships, for instance. We don't tend to them enough. And then, when we don't water them, we wonder why they wilt. But just like plants need water, human beings need it, too, and never more than when life takes a devastating turn.

Suffering from depression made this all too clear to me. I longed to know I mattered at a time when little did. I needed things from others that I couldn't give myself, like kindness, and assurance that the tunnel had an end.

But people don't like thinking that their loved ones are depressed, and often fail to understand the nature of the beast. That's why it's so common to see people turn away. Confusion and discomfort can make people disengage, leaving those who need support to face their fears alone.

Once I had some distance from my existential funk, I had more empathy for those whose lives took tragic turns. I vowed to act if I felt called to help in any way, and if it was appropriate, to lend a caring ear. I wanted to let others know they mattered, and were loved, and weren't viewed as a burden or as someone to avoid.

Marina's illness gave me my first chance to keep my word. *Just show up, and be yourself,* I thought. *Tune into love. Look her in the eyes, and let her show you what she needs. Don't assume you know what's best for her or how she feels. Do it in the way that you would like it done for you.*

Experience has taught me that when people are in need, presence is the greatest gift that we can ever give. There must be no agenda, though. Nor should we feel obliged. Instead, we must tread gently, with an open heart and mind.

TODAY, AS I recall the questions that Marina raised, it's clear to me that solving them had never been the point. Instead, we sought a window to a more coherent truth, through which we hoped to see some signs of life beyond the veil. But all we did was squint and shrug. Our window was too small. And there appeared to be no end to what we couldn't see.

Strangely, though, this eased some of our existential fear. Because so many things were imperceptible to us, it piqued our sense of how obscure the cosmic puzzle is. Obscure enough, perhaps, to harbor truths we couldn't grasp, like alternate realities where time does not exist. Or even one that we may come to know upon our death. To me, it's no less probable than our existence is. The magnitude of what we can't perceive is so immense that it would be naïve to think that wonders don't abound.

To entertain this notion might appear to be a leap, but this was also true when people thought the earth was flat. Surely, there are ways in which we're just as unaware. No one knows how we'll evolve and how our minds will bend, or even what we're capable of being conscious of.

The future of intelligence is artificial, though, so in due course we're likely to transcend our mind's constraints. And when we do, all bets are off. Imagine what we'll learn! Like how to eat the things we crave and not gain any weight. Or maybe that there's more to us than we can comprehend?

WHILE VISITING WITH friend and author Meggan Watterson, she asked what motivated me to write this kind of book. I told her that I thought the story would give people hope, but wondered if the details were too personal to share.

"What are you afraid of?" Meggan asked. "Can you explain?"

"I guess I'd like a thumbs-up from Marina," I replied.

"Okay, let's ask her then," she said, "since she likes sending signs! Let's ask for confirmation that this story should be told. In fact, let's do it now, okay? Marina . . . send a sign! And do it right away, so Michael doesn't question it!"

Right on cue, a glass flew from the table to the floor. I smiled inside as Meggan screamed.

"Well, look at that!" she squealed.

As Meggan plucked a napkin from amidst the broken glass, I listened as she pondered the significance of this.

"It's like a mitzvah!" Meggan said. "She's saying mazel tov! Your link to her was broken and reborn as something new! And now it can inspire you to do even greater things, like helping others understand that we survive our death. Perhaps you're writing this to help expose a greater truth? Or maybe it's a greater truth that has you writing this?"

As I sat down to process this, I had another thought. My mind flashed back to when Marina said she hoped to write and vowed to pen her story once she conquered her disease.

Of course, there also was her will. Here are the first two lines:

> *Someone should write a book from the journals I've kept over the past year, as well as incorporating other perspectives. Someone who feels passionate about the project should take it on, and do exactly what they feel is right with it.*

Sharon shared this with me once this book was underway. The truth was that I didn't know Marina had a will, nor did I have knowledge that this was what she proposed. It made me wonder if some part of her perceived her fate, and in effect was prepping me to yield to her request. Specifically, when she revealed her plan to write a book and seemed to be inviting me to play some kind of role. This might not sound like what a lucid person would suggest, but let's consider it at least, in light of what took place. What if there's a cyberspace for otherworldly mail, but we can only read it when we're able to respond? And what if we get insight or instructions in this mail, but it gets read and processed in a way we can't conceive? And what if, as some folks believe, there are contracts with souls, and we agree to work on things together on this plane? Or share experiences that allow us to evolve?

If all of this sounds fanciful, it did to me once too. And then I got those postcards from my dear departed niece.

WHEN I DISCUSS the details of this story in real life, it takes me by surprise sometimes when people shrug it off. It makes me wonder if they think I made the whole thing up, or if I told the story in an ineffective way.

Things that shift our paradigms are hard to take in stride. If something forces us to reconsider a belief, we can't just blink and calmly change the channel in our brain. We need some time to weigh and process what we're being told. Imagine switching from Fox News to MSNBC. A Fox News fan might disapprove of MSNBC, no matter what the hosts may say, or how sincere they are. And when the shoe is on the other foot, the same holds true.

Consider the resistance an election can provoke, and in particular the US presidential race. In the 2016 race, there was a clear divide, in which each party's biases were rigid and extreme. To each, the truth depended on the spins that they believed and rarely on perspectives gleaned from other points of view.

We saw this demonstrated in the O.J. Simpson case. The evidence was there. To some, it couldn't be denied. But jurors were assessing it with lenses that were fixed.

It's something to consider. Call it food for rigid thought. How often do you make things fit your version of what's true and disregard perspectives that you're unfamiliar with? Or feel compelled to judge a story like the one I've shared? If you're inclined to have beliefs—or judgments—that are fixed, it might be time to ask yourself how this is serving you. You can't live an enlightened life without a supple mind. Unless it can be bent a bit, you'll miss your greatest finds.

I hope this story gave you hope, and helped to stretch your mind. And that you'll look for postcards now. And find the ones you've missed.

Epilogue

Endings aren't my favorite thing to think or write about, but contemplating this one made me queasy from the start. In view of this, I hoped my niece might lend me some support. But since it was the two-year anniversary of her death, I also figured that she might have better things to do. *If not,* I thought, *she needs to get a better afterlife.*

And yet, with her track record, I was loath to rule it out.

WHEN I CALLED Sharon to reveal the subject of this book, I laughed when she suggested that Marina sowed the seed.

"Of course," I joked. "And knowing her, she'll help me write it too!"

But what I didn't know was that the joke would be on me. To my surprise, as I began to flesh the story out, her voice became increasingly coherent *in my head.*

Perhaps it is *her voice,* I thought, *in some discarnate sense?*
Except the skeptic in me needed more to be convinced.
Surely it's a stretch, I mused, *to think she'd guide my hand.*
Where she is now, she must have more important things to do.
Like preaching to the cosmic choir and mastering the harp. Or
paying off her karmic debt for frowning at my jokes!

But mystics say that there are few constraints in kingdom
come, and that in spirit, multitasking is a piece of cake. In
which case, souls can preach, play harps, pay debts, *and* ghost-
write books! In one fell swoop if space-time is as quantum as
we think.

WHILE SETTLING IN at Miraval, a health spa and resort,
memories of my prior stays were cycling through my mind.
This time, I was with Cheryl—who, for once, had nothing planned—my youngest brother, Chris, and his sweet-
tempered wife, Diane. I'd been there twice with Cheryl to
host workshops and retreats, but this time self-indulgence
was our focus. Nothing more.

While visiting with Wyatt Webb, an equine therapist, he
mentioned that a medium had been a hit with guests. For
several weeks, she had been doing readings at the spa, and
was receiving accolades for her impressive work. Of course, I
had the thought to book a session right away, but heard that
she had left and was unlikely to return.

I hurried to meet Cheryl, who was waiting at the pool.

"A medium was here," I said, while toppling her Thai tea.
"Anyway, I hear that she created quite a stir."

"Why don't you *call* her?" Cheryl said. "To see if she's still here!"

"I didn't think she would be."

"Would it hurt you to find out?"

"I heard that she was leaving."

"I'll call now."

"But—"

"I'm on hold."

"Thanks for trying, but I think—"

"She's free at 3 p.m.!"

"She is?"

"There was a cancellation right before I called!"

I met the medium, Tina, near the entrance to the spa. Without delay, she started to explain how we'd proceed, as well as what inspired her to pursue this line of work. The catalyst was something that she couldn't have conceived. It happened at a crash scene that she'd witnessed years before. She saw a man attempt to help a boy who had been hurt, but when she spoke to the police, the story took a turn. The man that she made reference to was nowhere to be found. No other witness saw him, and no cars had left the scene. And yet, she was convinced that she had seen him with the boy.

Later, she described the man—in detail—to police, who told her that she had portrayed the father of the child. And then, a short time later, she found out he was deceased. But not due to the accident. It happened long before.

I didn't dare let Tina know the reason I was there. I feared that if I did, it might inhibit our exchange. I also knew she could be swayed by gestures, nods, and grunts, and that if I suspected this, I'd question what she said.

I started getting fidgety as Tina settled in.

"There's someone coming through," she said. "Blood relative, I sense. Father's side? Grandmother? It's not her, but she's the link. Now I'm seeing *m-a-r*. Her name . . . is it *Marie*? She's saying she had cancer. Now I see the number two. Two years since she crossed over? Or two years that she was sick? She says you were her sounding board. Her voice of reason too. You offered insight . . . made her laugh. Does this make sense to you?"

"Is this a joke? Who told you this?"

"I hear this all the time."

"You do?"

"Hold on. She shows me a *balloon*. Was it a sign?"

"Did someone tell—"

"She says 'It's not just any old balloon!' She's laughing now. Do you know what this means? 'You *should*!' she says."

A vast array of expletives began to flood my mind. Thankfully, I had the sense to keep them to myself.

"She's been assisting you with an endeavor," Tina said. "Have you been writing something that the two of you discussed?"

"I have! This is—"

"She had a dog? It's with her. Was it black?"

"Yes! Her name was Sasha!"

"You play baseball? In a league?"

"I used to! Not that long ago. I'd like to try again!"

"'There is no try,' she says. 'Just *do*!' I love the way she laughs!"

"You can hear her laughing?"

"In a way, I can indeed! Now she's telling me you have an item that she made. She signed the front. It opens up. Is it some kind of card? She's saying it's her music. Now I'm seeing a CD."

"Yes! I have a—"

"Wait," she chuckled. "She has more to say! She says she's interrupting you because you talk too much!"

"Me? She can't be serious!"

"She says you're like . . . a pot? The pot that calls the kettle black? What does this mean to you?"

"It means that she's insufferable! And hasn't changed at all!"

"Again, she says that what you wrote was influenced by her. You're hoping that it will provide perspective, strength, and hope. She says it will for anyone that has an open mind. '*Whatever.*' She keeps saying that."

"She said it *all the time*!"

"Because of you, she actually looked forward to her death."

"A fair complaint."

"More laughter. She's enjoying your replies!"

"And still has the audacity to laugh at my expense!"

"She says you talked to her about what happens when we die. The insight you provided helped to take away her fear. She also says, 'When it's *your* turn, I'll be there, like you asked. To greet you.' But she says, 'Relax. It won't be for a while.'"

"Tell her that I love her, and she's missed!"

"Tell her yourself."

"She can hear me?"

"Yes, she can. She says she loves you too! She also wants to tell you that she's just a thought away. And that she even helped you to connect with me today!"

"It was improbable, for sure. In fact, I told my wife—"

"'Tell my mom and dad,' she says, 'I'm in a better place. Tell them that I love them, and can hear them think of me.'"

"I love her *more*! I want to hear about this better place!"

"'You'll know when it's your *turn* to know,' she says. 'For now, relax!'"

"Me? Relax? I'll need some help with that, as she should know!"

"She has a message. It's for you, and those who knew her well. 'Have fun,' she says. 'Tell *everyone*. Have fun! And don't hold back!'"

"She said this to her mother not too long before she passed!"

"Hold on. I'm getting something else. You have a bucket list?"

"Not one I've shared with anyone. Not even with my wife."

"Are you afraid that there are things you'll never get to do?"

"But how—"

"She says, 'Don't worry. You'll have all the time you need.'"

"I never mentioned this to her. Or anyone, in fact."

"She hears your thoughts."

"She . . . what? Is nothing sacred anymore?"

"She wants you to be kinder to yourself. And have more fun."

"It's going to be a challenge. Well, unless she plans to help."

"She says that there's no challenge you're unable to defeat."

"She might be right. Unless I'm challenged to accept defeat."

"You're quite a jokester, aren't you? I can see her nodding *yes*!"

"You see her nodding? She should talk! She was the queen of quips!"

"She just showed me the pot again."

"This joke is getting old!"

"I love this! She's suggesting that you're smarter than you seem. Perceptive too. In fact, a whole lot more than you appear."

"But aren't we *all* more than we seem?"

"Did she say that?"

"She did!"

"Again, she says she loves you."

"I love *you*!"

"You're very sweet."

"That was for *her*. You knew that, right?"

"No worries." Tina laughed.

"I see we're out of time," I sighed.

"To be continued, right?"

"I wish we *could* continue. I don't want to let her go!"

"'Then don't!' she says. 'Don't think of me as gone! Just out of sight!'"

"She said that? Really?"

"Yes indeed."

"She's quite a fluent ghost!"

"'Do all things with love,'" she says. 'With love you can't go wrong. Remember, love is everything. Believe that you are loved.'"

"All you need is love!" I laughed.

"Amen! The Beatles, right?"

"Marina loved the Beatles! *Love like ours can never die!*"

"She says, '*PS, I love you.*'"

"Hey, you're quick! Just like my niece!"

"Trust me, you can thank your niece. My wit is not that quick!"

"In keeping with the subject, *I don't want to leave her now.*"

"She's in your heart. Just think of her. It's—"

"*All I've got to do?*"

"'Yes!' she says. And you can do it—"

"*Any time at all?*"

"She's in agreement!" Tina chuckled. "Any time at all!"

So there's your happy ending. Who could ask for more than this? And yet, who says there won't be more? Not me. I'm staying tuned.

Cover art for compilation of Marina's tunes.
Includes credo ("more than we seem") and signature (above).

Postscript

After making final edits to the epilogue, a friend who I let read it had a curious response. Essentially, she wondered if I might have stretched the truth.

When I told Cheryl this, she asked me if I was surprised.

"I guess," I sighed. "You read it, though. How did it sound to you?"

"Why don't we let Marina be the judge?"

"You think?"

"Why not?"

"All right." I laughed. "Marina, help! I need another sign!"

And then, a minute later, both of us received a text. Our friend, Melissa, sent a link to an auspicious song. The title was "Marina." Jesse Terry penned the tune.

He wrote the song about a girl who died in 2012. In her graduation speech, five days before her death, Marina Keegan shared her vision for a happy life. "The Opposite of Loneliness" is what she called her speech. The lyrics could have easily been written for my niece!

Marina

Half a mural on her wall
Swirling sunsets, metallic stars
And she gets home late, just another night
Words stream out above streetlights

I picture her far-off stare
She could have gone anywhere
Instead she's bouncing off all the satellites
Some things never will die
Oh Marina

Oh my the song comes slow
For a face I did not know
For some words now etched in stone and in my mind
Oh my I must confess
I hate to see the light like this
The opposite of loneliness is where I am
Oh Marina, why'd you have to go
Why'd you have to go

Amber hair in a photograph
She's tryin' hard not to laugh
I woke up today feelin' so damn young
Free to go where the muse may run
Oh Marina

Oh my the song comes slow
For a face I did not know
For some words now etched in stone and in my mind
Oh my I must confess

I hate to see the light like this
The opposite of loneliness is where I am
Oh Marina

Thanks for passing through my friend
I swear I'll always look ahead
It's all that matters in the end

CHORUS

JESSE TERRY
JACKSON BEACH MUSIC (SESAC) 2012

Acknowledgments

Brian Weiss, MD

Meggan Watterson

Bob Olson

Melissa Olson

Curt Gerrish

Pat Gerrish

Anne Frances Hardy

Beth Platow

Alexandra Oliver

Kelly Notaras

Elisabeth Rinaldi

Kristen Weber

Bruce Kohl

Risa Rodil

Shannon Littrell

Lisa Fugard

Lisa Sundstrom

Tina Powers

Rita Heron

Ileen Maisel

Cheryl Richardson

Mike Day

Sharon Day

Marina Day

About the Author

Michael Gerrish lives in Massachusetts with his wife, Cheryl Richardson. To inquire about his private sessions and events, contact him at michael@michaelgerrish.com or lisa@michaelgerrish.com.

AUTHOR'S CONTACT INFORMATION:
Michael Gerrish
PO Box 205
West Newbury, MA 01985
USA

michael@michaelgerrish.com

Other Books by Michael

When Working Out Isn't Working Out:
A Mind/Body Guide to Conquering
Unidentified Fitness Obstacles.
St. Martin's Press, 1999.

The Mind-Body Makeover Project:
A 12 Week Guide for Transforming
Your Body and Life.
McGraw-Hill, 2003, 2004.

CPSIA information can be obtained
at www.ICGtesting.com
Printed in the USA
LVHW010158100221
678885LV00003B/332